# BE THE LIGHT

## A True Story of Good Overcoming Evil

GITA JAIRAJ

A catalogue record for this book is available from the British Library.

This book is available at Christian bookstores and distributors worldwide.

ISBN: 978-1-5272-4793-2

Printed in the United Kingdom.

# DEDICATION

This book is dedicated to my Lord and Saviour Jesus Christ. Who, through His love, mercy and grace kept me, so that I may have life and have it more abundantly.

# ACKNOWLEDGEMENTS

The last few years have seen my faith tested to its limits. I would like to thank God first and foremost for giving me strength and power. I am still standing and am so grateful for the insights and blessings that are now raining down on me.

To my parents, Dr. M and Mrs R. Jairaj, for their love and limitless generosity. They are the best parents. I am so blessed to be their daughter.

To the rest of my beautiful family – love and thanks.

To Azania and her amazing team, Rebecca, Ray, John, Kim and Al-Photography.

My deepest gratitude to the tireless men and women of God who literally saved my life and got me back on my life's path, Pastor D and Pastor B, RM, Louis, Kristina and Akua. Thank you for your powerful prayer warriorship.

I am so grateful to my church, Holy Trinity Brompton, Knightsbridge, under the amazing stewardship of Nicky and Pippa Gumble and their team including Tom Simpson, Stephen Foster and Sarah Cook. And to my Connect Group(s) KCG and Walker especially Ros, Alex, Donna P, Charis and Elsa for the invaluable fellowship and support.

Cashmore - for always being there.

Massive thanks to Raymond Aaron, Liz Ventrella, Danielle Stevens and team.

To my mentors, Tony Dada, Brother Ishmael Tetteh, Raymond Aaron, Simon Rogers and Graham W. Price. I thoroughly appreciate all that I am learning from you. You raise my game. Deep gratitude.

I am also incredibly blessed to have Helena Shenel as my dear friend and the best vocal coach there is. You helped me find my voice.

I deeply appreciate all of my previous music managers and collaborators, some of whom are my dear friends, Tony Ponte (RIP), Tony Stafford (RIP), Dave Woolf, Val and Jane Risdon, Sheen Doran, Alan Seifert, Andy Grant, Dipak Patel, Charles Bailey, Danny Chang and Colin Edwards for your guidance and creativity in matters musical.

I would like to greatly acknowledge Peter Ferris, Ajay Joshi (RIP), Ria Richardson (RIP), Linzy Attenborough, Sarah Berger, Bernard Hiller, Stewart Pearce, Chris Rozanski and the teachers at Birmingham Theatre School. David Vann (RIP) and teachers at The Birmingham School of Acting for teaching me invaluable skills over the years. Not forgetting Equity, the actors' union for all the hard work they do. Also, Simon Furness and the Actors Temple.

My wonderful friends;

Dawn, Karen, Ali, Cath, Leb, Vicky, Ze, Nikki, Lisa, Effie, Donna G, Earnest, Gwyneira, The Newman family, Rajais, Balbira, Magda, Annie, Angus, Noreen, Galia, Angela, Padma, Kavita, Lou, Dimitri, Sib Elle, Eija, Claire, Doc Susy and Khush, and my fund raising and gym buddies too numerous to mention individually. Thank you for your love and support through thick and thin.

# CONTENTS

# FOREWORD
## BY
## RAYMOND AARON

Be the Light by Gita Jairaj is a powerful and thought-provoking true story.

Gita has taken on a subject that few people talk about openly and that is surrounded by controversy. For that I applaud her. Have you found yourself in a position where life was generally happy and peaceful, then suddenly events unfold in ways which are inexplicable? Everything seems to be going wrong, relationships, career, health and finances. This can be happening to you regardless of race, faith or creed. You are left questioning everything. Gita tells her story in such a way that engages your emotions with moments of laughter and palpable sadness. It was her simple faith, determination and perseverance that saw her through.

Maybe you are facing similar challenges. This book may lead to examination of what is occurring in your life in a new way. One where you recognise that other forces are at play. What happens in the spiritual universe can impact the physical in major ways. Gita shares her story to encourage you not to be afraid and to never give up regardless of your circumstances. Help is at hand. Let her be the catalyst to direct you. There is light. Follow it with your heart and you too can find your way out of the darkness into the light.

# CHAPTER 1

## THE DISCOVERY 2013

"You need to come back now."

Pietro's voice was urgent, panicked even. I was at a friend's, Sarita's beauty salon in Clapham. She was having a promotion on some of her products. This coincided with a street party which was in full swing. It was a beautiful day and I was in a good mood. I was happy where I was and didn't want to go anywhere.

"What is it?" I asked grumpily."

"I found something, you need to come back right now," he insisted. There was no arguing with his tone. So, I said my goodbyes and jumped into the car and drove back to Kings Road as fast as I could. All sorts of things were going through my mind. It was on overdrive. I got to Kings Road, parked badly and ran into the building, up the stairs and into his showroom. My husband's face was pale and clearly upset. "Look at these," as he opened his hand and sitting in the palm of his hand were two rat shaped voodoo dolls. Everything went into slow motion. All I remember was staring at them for what seemed like ages. One part of me couldn't believe it and the other part completely understood.

3

The two effigies, one was a male rat and the other was a female, were made of material that appeared to be very old. They were about two to two and a half inches in height. The male rat was wearing a suit and a little hat, and the female was wearing a full-length dress with a waistcoat over the top. I was furious, this confirmed everything that I had been feeling and thinking about, all the bad energy and strange feelings. I knew there was something anchoring all of this to the showroom and why things were never right no matter how hard we tried. I asked Pietro where he had found them. He told me that they were in a vase which was part of a set that he had just sold to a client a few days ago. He had discovered the dolls while preparing the vases for packaging.

There were two vases and a central piece. They were a beautiful Scandinavian brand. Thick, heavy, round bottomed vases which graduated into long slender necks with a narrow opening at the top. The glass was black with a white stripe running up each side. He had been wrapping them up for the client to collect. As he had turned one vase upside down, he noticed something coming out of the top. He thought it was just a little bit of material that had somehow made its way inside. He pulled at it, and got a big shock when the rat voodoo doll came out in its entirety. Now alerted that something had been inside that vase he shook it and realized something else was in there. There was another voodoo doll, this time it was the female rat doll. The glass was not transparent, so heaven knows how long these horrible objects had been sitting in there.

After taking in what I saw sitting in his hand I told him to give them to me as I was going to go next door and ram them down that old-bags throat. It was hard to control the intense burning anger I felt at that moment. The three years of hell we had been subjected to compounded into that one moment. Pietro had to physically hold me back from charging next door to sort out the owner of that showroom and his partner. He said, "They mustn't know that we have found them." It took quite a while to calm me down! We decided to call one of our Christian mentors and advisor, Pastor

4

B, for advice about what to do with the effigies. The phone call was brief and animated with the instruction coming down the line that we should burn them asap. The hardest thing to do was to remain silent and pretend that nothing had happened. We had to interact with our neighbours as normal. Pietro spoke to one of his friends, Gareth, that he trusted about what he had found and they both arranged a time to meet and go to the Gasworks, which is an area behind the Kings Road where they burnt the voodoo dolls and flushed the remaining ashes down a drain. They had to make sure they were destroyed.

# CHAPTER 2

—×( )×—

# LIVING THE LIFE

## HOW I MET MY HUSBAND

Let me take you back to the beginning.

In 2004 my parents, myself and a good friend of theirs from the tennis club, James, decided to take a 6-week road trip to Australia. In all the time I had been with Greg, my Australian ex-fiancé, they had never visited Australia with me. I was excited to finally get the opportunity to do this with them as I love Australia so much. James had been traveling to Australia for the last few years for three months at a time with his wife, who had sadly passed away a couple of years prior to this. This was the first time he was going back without her and he wanted to do this with friends.

We had the most wonderful time starting in Sydney and slowly driving up the East Coast. We got to Noosa, which is my favourite resort in Australia. We stayed at a boutique hotel-belonging to James's friends, the Smiths. They had two daughters, Anne and Coral, we all spent time together doing BBQs and little trips locally. The icing on the cake was that my old friends Lucy and George from the UK who had emigrated to Australia with their two sons and had settled in Brisbane many years before joined us and booked into our resort to spend time with us. That was a road trip to cherish.

7

A few years later, in the summer of 2008, Anne wanted to visit London. I arranged for her to stay at my sister's house in North London. We decided the easiest way to see the sights of London was by The Big Bus company. We spent one Saturday hopping on and off the bus taking in all the tourist attractions, Buckingham Palace, The Houses of Parliament, The London Eye etc. It was a very enjoyable but tiring day. By the evening we felt it was time to relax with a glass of wine. I called another girlfriend, Lily and told her to meet us at my favourite local wine bar, Brinkley's. Being summer it was jam packed as usual. Eventually we got a table by the window enjoying the breeze and chatting away.

After a while I noticed that two men at the bar, one fair haired and the other one was Latin, dark haired, good looking, were looking at us trying to get our attention. One waved, I looked over briefly, smiled and carried on chatting to my friends. Half an hour later, Bill another friend of mine came into the bar and joined us. Within a few minutes of that a smart black man, had joined the two men at the bar who continued to try to get our attention. This third guy, to break the ice came over to Bill and started a conversation with him about his shoes of all things. They both had handmade shoes by the same designer and had spent a silly amount on them. It's not only women who have a thing about shoes it seems! His name was Charles, and this was then the cue for the two men at the bar to finally come over to us.

The fair haired one was called Andrew and the Latin one was Pietro. He was Italian. There was an instant connection between Pietro and me. We talked a great deal and we made each other laugh. We all stayed drinking champagne until the bar closed and decided to go to a local club, Catch 22 I think it was called back then. Pietro and I became inseparable that evening and we hit the dance floor. He could dance, a bonus. Charles-had a bit too much to drink and was getting flirty and pushy with me. Pietro didn't like this and became protective, so I thought. This I later discovered was his possessive streak. All good things must come to an end and it had been a great evening. Pietro then had to make sure that Andrew got home safely as he had suddenly decided to leave, and Pietro was worried about him drinking and driving so he had to go after him. He said he didn't want to leave me. He had held my hand tightly for a lot of the evening. This felt natural even though I had just met him. We exchanged numbers and he said he would call me the next day. Which he did. I was heading back to Birmingham to stay with my parents. I was recovering from a split with my former boyfriend and I always found staying with my parents at such times comforting. I was taking Anne with me and we were getting ready for the drive North when Pietro called and said he really had to see me before I went to Birmingham.

We met briefly at lunchtime before I went back. To say it was a whirlwind romance is an understatement. I didn't tell my family about him at first, I just wanted to enjoy it and see what happened. I had met Pietro nine months after I had split from my previous partner Liam, which had been a difficult journey. The only thing about Pietro was that I found him to be mysterious when I first met him. He told me he had split up with his former partner, Janet a little while before I had met him. I wasn't sure where he lived. I didn't find out for the first couple of weeks as he was being vague.

Eventually he told me he was still living at Janet and her mother's house until he found another flat. I was a bit concerned by this, but he reassured me, and I felt he was being genuine. He said he had his own room and it was amicable. I believed him, maybe I was being naive. However, very soon after he took over a flat belonging to his friend. At the beginning Janet would call him crying and asking him to come back to her. I was trying to be understanding at first but then it started to annoy me. I wasn't sure if he had told her he had met someone else. Something I learnt as I got older is that honesty is always the best policy. I admit that wasn't always the case and I was a bit of nightmare when I was younger and was creative with the truth when it came to men! Things come back to bite you and it isn't worth it in the end. The law of cause and effect. Thank goodness I had changed.

In no uncertain terms I told him he was to sort it out and just tell her. Either way she told him that someone had seen him with this Indian girl. So, she knew about me and found out my name. The calls stopped and I thought things would settle down. We spent all our time together. It was intense. After three and a half months Pietro asked me to marry him. I said yes. This surprised even me as my nickname used to be the 'runaway bride' because I used to be afraid of commitment. What can I say? I was always a free spirit.

## MARRIED LIFE

We are both very close to our families. My parents are the most generous, kind and loving parents. I am biased, however. My siblings and myself are incredibly blessed. They never interfered in our choice of partners. We didn't have arranged marriages inflicted upon us. The closest we got was when my maternal grandmother, Umuma, would send photos of Indian doctors to us from India to see if we liked any of them. My older sister and I would giggle as they were very geeky and looked like they had half of jar of coconut oil slicking their hair down in a centre parting. Not a good look for us. We were free to make our own choices. My two sisters and brother married English partners. I was marrying an Italian. My family were very surprised when I told them I was getting married. None of them had even met Pietro. I had only known him for several weeks when he had proposed. My family, as any other family would do, suggested that we should get to know each other better before rushing into marriage. After a bit of persuasion my parents were happy that I was getting married at last.

They welcomed Pietro with open arms and treated him like a son. My mum said she was happy that Pietro was clipping my wings! When I was younger marriage and children never appealed to me as I loved travelling and disliked too much responsibility. Having said that I was meant to marry a handsome Australian called Greg, 10 years before this in St Lucia. It was all booked, some of my friends even went despite the cancellation because they had already paid for the trip. It got called off because Greg thought I wouldn't move to Australia and that it would end in divorce. He was right. As it turned out, I subsequently signed with a new music manager and had told him I was going back to England. So, it would never have worked. It broke my heart, but my career beckoned, and I think he was a bit scared of marriage as he was still young. We remain friends today.

Pietro became close to my parents and he suggested several times that as my parents were getting older, we should encourage them to move to London and we should get a place together so that we could help look after them. My parents were very touched by that. We would enjoy our frequent visits to them in Birmingham.

Things progressed at speed and we were married within nine months of meeting in 2008. There was a lot of going backwards and forwards to Rome for the correct documentation and formalities. We spent a great deal of time with Pietro's parents, Riccardo and Bettina, making all the arrangements. They were very kind and helpful. The wedding was in Rome, an intimate ceremony. At the Caracalla, a beautiful, former ornate church, Santa Maria in Tempula. This is just behind the Colosseum. My family were there and only a couple of close friends from the UK, Terry and Eala. Pietro's family and some of his Italian friends who couldn't come to the UK celebration attended.

We all piled into two buses which were arranged by Pietro's lovely cousin, Viola, who was a policewoman and one of her friends who was a senior policewoman. I found this cool, it felt like we had our own police escort. They drove us 60 kilometres to a fabulous, well known restaurant by a lake owned by friends of Pietro's family near Ronciglione, a picture-perfect small town, where his parents lived. This was followed a month later by an extravagant blessing in Birmingham. This took place at St. George's my old school church where my two sisters had been married and The Hyatt Regency in Birmingham Broad Street.

We had a great life. Pietro was very loving and kind, I felt so blessed. I had spent over 20 years as a medical representative for various pharmaceutical companies such as Pfizer and I had decided to retire very early. However, Pietro had started his business in a large emporium in Kings Road and rents are very high there. So, I would help in the showroom and I took a part time job in the charity fundraising sector. This was very flexible and enabled me to be able to travel to Italy 4-6 times a year with Pietro to source the beautiful pieces for his showroom. I used to love those trips. We would travel through France, Belgium, Holland, Germany, Austria and through to Italy.

In London we had an active social life and would be out eating, drinking and partying usually in Kings Road or Pimlico area with my friends or Pietro's colleagues in the antique and design business. I got caught up in married life and my aspirations in music and acting were put on hold. To be honest I had become a bit disillusioned with the politics of the entertainment business and all the previous years of the casting couch scenario. I never put up with any of that nonsense. That's a whole other story.

## THE GREEN-EYED MONSTER

My siblings, Rena, Shiloh, Jay and I had a happy childhood growing up in Birmingham. Apart from teenage tantrums and having Asian parents who were very protective and tried to be strict with us. My father was a respected doctor, both grandfathers were doctors. So, we grew up in an affluent, middle class home. My father used a lot of his income to send all four of us to private school, we were members of the Edgbaston Priory Tennis Club and went on nice holidays. Our house was an open house to our friends. My friends would often stay for several days, and my mother's curries were famous. My parents were incredibly generous with everyone. It was usually mum who was responsible for disciplining us. Dad was the quiet one. When he did say something, you knew you were in trouble. However, he did spoil us on occasion. When we used to get taken shopping as kids, we would try to separate mum and dad because we knew dad would spoil us and buy us more clothes. In department stores mum would go off to look for what she wanted and poor dad was left exposed. I had a knack of getting dad to buy me three or four items of clothing whereas mum may have only got me one. She used to roll her eyes but would let me get away with it. I took this for granted until one day a school friend was staying the weekend with us and we went into town with my parents to do some shopping.

The above scenario took place and I remember dad bought me about four dresses. I noticed my friend was very quiet and looked a bit upset. It only dawned on me then that I had been insensitive as my friend lived in a vicarage and that maybe this was not something that her parents could or would do. That had a big impact on me. I decided that wouldn't happen again and that it would be better to consider situations more carefully. I was grateful and mindful that I had good friends but also there were certain people who had pretended to be friends and were bad mouthing us to other people. Which I found incredibly disappointing and upsetting. You soon find out who your real friends are. I learned to be wary from a young age. I only have a handful of friends from that period who are still my true, cherished friends now. They have supported me through thick and thin. You know who you are!

My older sister and I were always interested in fashion from the age of 12 or 13 years old and we had a fantastic dressmaker called Miss Heppenstall. She was in her 70s when we first used to go to her with copies of Vogue clutched tightly in our hands, along with material (usually my mother's prized silk saris!) to copy the elaborate designs in its glossy pages. She had been a designer at the department store Rackhams in Birmingham for a very long time. There was nothing she couldn't make. This was supplemented with trips to Biba on Kensington High Street with Toyah Wilcox who was my sister's close friend at school. We would get kitted out in pencil skirts and pillbox hats at the age of 14. Real brats, we wanted to make ourselves look older. Looking back at old photos I looked about 30! And typically, now I am trying hard to look younger…

Looking back those were good, simple times. We would stay at Toyah's house some weekends and she would come to ours. Her parents would spend time on their boat in Pershore and we were left to our own devices. My parents didn't know that bit. We would go into town and go clubbing and have the occasional party at her house. We were quite well behaved, nothing got out of hand. I remember trying to be sophisticated drinking Campari and soda/ lemonade because of the Campari adverts at the time with Lorraine Chase. I didn't even like it, I was just posing. All three of us used to do quite a bit of that.

It's fair to say my sister and I were the first Asian girls who dressed the way we did and were on the Birmingham scene. Because we were considered a bit exotic and ahead in the fashion stakes, there was no shortage of guys wanting to get to know us. It got us into many fights with their irate girlfriends and we hadn't done anything wrong and we didn't encourage them. Most of the time we wouldn't touch their guys with a barge pole, but the rumour mill was working overtime. I said most of the time but there was one guy, James, when I first met him, his ex, Lynn wouldn't accept it was over with him and would try and make my life hell. She nicknamed me, "the Star of Asia!" Lynn and her cronies would often pick fights in bars and clubs around town. They would start fights but it wouldn't end well for them! It sounds funny now, but it wasn't at the time. I often went home having to hide scratches and bruises and occasionally torn clothes! My mother could always tell when I had been in a fight the night before and that I had been crying because in the morning my eyes would be puffy. I didn't give in to their bullying.

Bullying. This is an important subject especially nowadays and with the added layer of social media. Before its advent at least you knew who and what you are up against but now people hide behind "the veil." Thankfully awareness has been raised and systems finally being put in place to protect the vulnerable especially children of school age. My advice to kids today especially girls is to take up self-defence classes which will give them mental strength and confidence.

In my experience the bullying intensified when I met my Noah. I was still at college and he came from a well-off middle-class family, had a sports car and looked like a young Marlon Brando. There was also an edge to it as Asian men didn't like to see Asian women with Caucasian men and would pick fights. You couldn't win.

I did have a bit of a reputation for being able to take care of myself. My family and friends came first and would be protected fiercely. So, jealousy was a recurring theme in my and my family's life. Pietro and I were a very close couple. He would always hold my hand tightly wherever we were, at dinner, in the pub or wherever we went. Our friends would comment on it. My friends when they saw us together, they would often tell me afterwards that Pietro would always look at me adoringly. They said we made a great couple. But we were also known to be possessive of each other and that would cause fireworks on occasion. He was a typical fiery Italian and his temper was an issue at times. However, we had a strong, happy relationship. Pietro would often say that some people were jealous of our relationship and of what we had. He always kept saying we had to protect ourselves.

# CHAPTER 3

—— ✕ ☐ ✕ ——

# THE EARLY DAYS

## INITIAL OPPOSITION

How we ever got married in the first place is a miracle. From the onset of our relationship in 2008 there was a definite energy interference. Pietro's ex, Janet, as I mentioned earlier had been very upset when he ended their relationship. She had wanted Pietro to marry her. Janet's family were from the Caribbean and I had my suspicions or a knowing that she was using juju and that she was behind things going wrong with where we were living, with the business and our health. Pietro started getting the most excruciating back pain it felt as if he was being repeatedly stabbed. He would be confined to bed for periods of time and not be able to move. This had a big impact on his work. He was a sole trader and had to be fit and able to conduct his business or he would lose money. On one occasion at about 8 o'clock in the evening, he was in so much pain he literally couldn't move a muscle, he was lying on his back and his back was in complete spasm. We were both scared. I had never seen him this bad before. I tried everything to help him but, in the end, I had to call the emergency GP service number. They just went through a list of questions that went on for more than 20 minutes and to be honest they were not very helpful in this instance whereas they had been in the past. They probably thought I was exaggerating. I decided to call my dad who said that it would be best to get him to Birmingham straightaway. With superhuman strength that came from above I managed to get him into his van. I was also very aware that it contained some very expensive items, chandeliers and furniture that he hadn't had time to unload beforehand, plus we weren't expecting this situation. I drove as fast as I could up the motorway to my parent's house in Birmingham. There was a lot of crashing about in the back of the van, Pietro was in too much pain to care whether his beautiful goods were getting smashed to smithereens or not!

Once in Birmingham dad called his friend, Doctor M, who had bought dad's surgery after he had retired and asked him to see Pietro first thing in the morning. Doctor M examined Pietro and gave him the documentation so that he would be seen without having to wait at Dudley Road hospital's A & E department for hours. He was seen straight away at the X-ray department and he was given scans plus serious pain killers. We then went back to my parent's house and I quickly arranged for him to see a specialist who was a close friend of my former partner who had also been a GP. I knew that once we were in Birmingham, we could get to see the relevant doctors without having to mess around or wait too long. After the examination of the X-rays and scans, there was really nothing physically wrong with Pietro as we both knew already. He was treated for severe back pain and spasm and he was given very strong painkillers and muscle relaxants. Crazy as it may sound to some people (but I add, not to others) we both had the idea or suspicion that it was all down to Janet sticking pins into an effigy of Pietro. I am being completely serious. Pietro is extremely intuitive, and my instincts are rarely wrong.

## THE SHOWROOM

Pietro's family came from a line of glass and furniture manufacturers on the paternal side and the military and police on his maternal side. One of his aunts was made the first female General in the Italian army. It was headline news in Italy. Pietro is the spitting image of his paternal grandfather. He had a great work ethic which Pietro inherited, and he made a fortune in the manufacturing industry. Unfortunately, a lot of family money was lost many years later in a family battle once he had died and the business was dissipated. Pietro opened his first showroom at the age of 17 in Bari, Italy. He later opened a second showroom. His parents decided to move to Rome and Pietro made the move later. Before I met him, he had been going backwards and forwards to Italy doing business and he had split up with his partner in Rome and had met Janet in the UK. He sold his chandeliers and various items to other dealers around London. He also dealt from a couple of Emporiums in Islington and Kings Road.

Once we got married, he wanted to establish himself properly in the UK and have his own dedicated showroom in London as he had previously done in Bari. I encouraged him and told him to apply for a loan to secure a lease in one of the showrooms in the big emporium on Kings Road. The opportunity arose because a lease had just become available for a showroom on the first floor that was owned by a colleague. The loan was approved, and Pietro bought the lease for his showroom. The lease and related documents had to be looked over which was tedious. However, my background is in law, I just managed to get a law degree and do the Solicitors Final Exams in which I only got 5 of the 7 heads because law was something I never wanted to study in the first place. In truth it was my parents' choice. However, it has come in useful over the years and it did save Pietro money as I could do some of the preliminary work checking the lease and contracts. We then got a property lawyer to check and finalise everything.

This was 2010 and a proud moment. Pietro had his showroom a few months after us getting married. Now the hard work of knocking it into shape started. The space was dark and gloomy with rust colour wall coverings. This all had to be ripped off and everything was painted white. It became fresh and clean and my husband's Italian chandeliers sparkled beautifully. He is an expert in Italian 20th century design. The furniture was very elegant and the buzz around the showroom made us anticipate business would be very good. Prospective clients came in and expressed great interest in the various pieces. This emporium is well known and royalty, pop stars, actors and celebrities would regularly come in and buy the beautiful pieces from the different showrooms in the building. You would regularly see bodyguards stationed throughout the building when the Queen of this country and the Prince of that country would come to the building. The Queen of a particular European country used to come in regularly. The first time she came in I had no idea who she was, she came with another lady and there were no obvious bodyguards. I popped my head over the mezzanine floor's bannister and said as I usually did, "If you need any help, just let me know." She liked one or two of the pieces. When she left one of the girls from the showroom next door said, "Did you know that was the Queen of so and so country." I wasn't fazed just pleasantly surprised how ordinary and nice she was, with no airs and graces. You know that's how people should be. This was in sharp contrast to another client of the emporium, a Prince of a Far Eastern country who liked a bit of a fanfare. He was about to come into Pietro's when I was told I would have to curtsey and that he didn't like people to look him in the eyes. Well that was it. There would be no curtsey from me and if he spoke to me, I would look at him directly. This was made clear. So, I was bundled up to the mezzanine floor because it was too late to get me out of the way and the other dealers on the first floor were worried, I would be 'disrespectful' and cause a scene. I was annoyed at the time, but to this day it bemuses me. It was so ridiculous.

## THE NEIGHBOURS

I clearly remember the lukewarm reception from the neighbour who owned the showroom on the same floor, on the left-hand side of the building. The emporium has about 20 showrooms inside it mainly selling furniture and decorative art. It is set in a rectangle around a little central courtyard. It has 2 floors, a bar, a nightclub and there is a restaurant in the basement. This neighbour on the left was called Ken and he had a German partner call Helga. Ken appeared pleasant enough, but Helga was a very cold fish. No one in the building liked her. Just before I appeared on the scene Ken had left his wife Sarah of 25 to 30 years to be with this woman Helga. Apparently, everyone liked Sarah and thought Ken had behaved atrociously to his wife. Keep this in mind for future reference. Helga was supposed to be an energy worker and healer. That's how Ken had met her. He had had an injury, somehow, he found Helga and went to have a session with her. A relationship developed and the story goes he literally moved her into part of the barn conversion he owned with his wife in the countryside while his wife was still there! Sarah had to endure this for months before she moved up North to stay with her mother. She was also displaced in the showroom. She had helped her husband build the business for years yet in a very short time Helga had taken over. This had shocked the other dealers. Pietro disliked Helga and was disgusted with Ken's behaviour as he knew and liked Sarah. He used to recount the story frequently and reiterate that Ken was a nasty man.

## TACTICS

I am usually a good judge of character. I say usually as a caveat because sometimes we can get it wrong. When it came to Helga and to some extent Ken, I didn't get it wrong. Helga was not nice, she attempted to act superior and came across just plain rude. She claimed to be an energy and bodywork expert. She had an unpleasant energy and I would not let her put her hands on me however much she would try to persuade me to have a session with her. No thank you. From the start there was this insidious hostility emanating from the pair. They would say one thing to you but do something else. Two faced.

The emporium is a bit of a maze with showrooms tucked into corners. Pietro's showroom was slightly set back. Back then you could only approach it from two sides after going up a staircase on the left from the ground floor and turning either left or right at the top of it. It could only be accessed via going through other showrooms. There was no direct access. To reach it you had to go through two on the left and one on the right. This has since changed. A gangway has been built to give direct access to Pietro's showroom. In those days it was hard to get clients to even reach Pietro's. All sorts of tactics were being used to prevent this. Why? I can hear you say. The competition was fierce in that building and cutthroat. The Recession hit badly in 2008. People were precious about clients and didn't like their clients going and doing business with the other dealers. Quite ridiculous as there should be enough for everyone and people have different tastes and ideas. Having said this there was quite a lot of brown furniture in the building. Traditional antiques. Don't get me wrong some of it was very beautiful. But some was very bland. Pietro's pieces were different and a totally different period. There is nothing like Italian design, past or present. Twentieth Century design is particularly stunning and desirable. A couple of the other dealers would try to copy his style or acquire similar pieces, but they didn't have the requisite knowledge as to what was an original or fake. Pietro knew the work of e. g. Osvaldo Borsani, Gio Ponti, Paolo Buffa and Venini.

As I said when the showroom opened there was a lot of interest and people were talking about Pietro's goods and interior designers were coming from all over the place. However, in the first three months of the showroom being open Pietro only sold one Murano glass bowl for £120! Rents on the Kings Road are not cheap. Obviously, we were worried. It was very strange because so many people would come in and say they loved the chandeliers and the furniture, and that they were very interested in purchasing them and to even invoice them. Then nothing. They would disappear or say they had changed their minds and didn't want the items anymore. This would become a recurring theme. One chandelier comes to mind, at the time it was over £100, 000, came through a colleague and was from one of Versace's houses. An interior designer had come in three times and was acting for an Arab princess. She came in the third time with the designer, everything was agreed, and Pietro sent an invoice. We were waiting for the payment and to pack it up, but nothing happened. The princess was worth many billions, it wasn't as if she couldn't afford it. We also had this strong feeling that people couldn't see that the showroom was there. They would literally walk past it as if it didn't exist at all. It was like an invisible barrier had gone up.

We knew something was happening on an energetic and spiritual level. Ken and Helga would constantly light incense in their showroom, clang Tibetan cymbals in there and chant. She would sometimes come into Pietro's and make herself comfortable on one of his sofas and close her eyes and seem to meditate for a few minutes. I told him to throw her out when she did this because I knew exactly what she was trying to do. He wouldn't, and he wouldn't let me do it either. He wanted to keep the peace. This, in retrospect, prolonged our suffering. I should have done it

Things were happening in the physical realm too. Ken and Helga would put up physical blocks to stop people getting through to Pietro's. It was all made to look very innocent. A ladder would be put in front of the exit of their showroom into the common parts preventing clients from entering Pietro's. Or rows of chairs blocking that entrance whenever the wealthy Chinese clients would come into the building. Sometimes Helga would come into the showroom and interrupt Pietro when he was right in the middle of talking to clients or doing a sale. That was particularly aggravating. Ken would physically stand in front of clients with his back to the entrance of Pietro's to block them going next door or talking to them for far too long, usually gibberish until they got bored and wanted to leave the building quickly, not even making it next door. These two would also direct clients to other stores in Kensington Church Street or Pimlico for certain pieces that they knew Pietro had in stock. They weren't the only ones guilty of directing clients away from Pietro, a couple of other dealers in the building used to do this too.

Another worry was that big scratches would appear on some of Pietro's furniture, usually his dining tables and especially after he had had them professionally polished or had new glass tops put on them at great expense. We had our suspicions, but this time we didn't think it was only down to Ken or Helga. In the end a very expensive security camera had to be put in. The table scratching stopped thankfully but the bad energy did not. This didn't stop at the showroom-Pietro's van would get scratched or sprayed. It was sprayed with gold paint on one occasion when it was parked outside our flat. My car would get the odd scratch, flat tyres and damaged wing mirrors.

# CHAPTER 4

——————×〔〕×——————

# UNITED FRONT

With all this going on and from previous experience I already knew something wasn't right. In those days I was a nominal Christian. I had gone with my two sisters to a private girls' school, Edgbaston Church of England College for Girls. Our church was St. Georges church, as a child I went to church occasionally and prayed when I needed something or was in trouble. In my teens I flirted with Buddhism and New Age after that. Spiritualist healing captured my interest and I had started going for healing and readings.

My mother is a devout Christian and she nagged me not to go for readings as she said they were against God and the Christian faith. I told her they were harmless and to stop nagging and I carried on. I also started having my Tarot cards read and clairvoyance sessions on a regular basis. I was hooked on trying to find out what my future held. Over a period of many years I was happy to mix this all in with my Christianity and made good friends with a few of the people I consulted. I went regularly to the SAGB, (Spiritualist Association of Great Britain, of which Arthur Conan Doyle (author of Sherlock Holmes fame) had been a supporter. I went when it was in Belgrave Square for healing and a lead healer there, Big G invited me to join her development circle, which I did and was a member for a couple years. I already could see and just 'knew' about certain things. The circle would go and do a night giving readings at the local community hall near Big G's once every few weeks. It could get busy on those nights with quite a few people coming in for insight. The six of us circle members would do sand, psychometry and flower readings which would be spot on most of the time. I decided to leave the group because I was seeing things I didn't want to see.

I will just say I have been the target of many spiritual attacks and I have done my best to help others who have also been attacked in the same way. People seem to gravitate towards me and ask for help when the supernatural is involved. However, in reflection, I was not qualified to delve in these matters, it really is a dark world, and the fact is you cannot serve two masters. I did not realise this at the time. This was one of the reasons that prompted me to finally write this book.

For many years I went to four different people Zaelia, Eric, Gaynor and Big G. I trusted them to help me spiritually and give me guidance as to my future. When things were confusing or going wrong, I would go to see them. I would see them when things were going well too, and I had to make an important decision on a certain situation or was at a crossroads. This is not anything unusual as it is well documented that certain Heads of State, Presidents and of course Princess Diana were known for consulting clairvoyants, psychics and astrologers. Some prominent people won't make major moves without consulting their spiritual advisors. Whenever I felt I was under major spiritual attack or weird things would be happening I would consult my advisors or pop down the road to the College of Psychic Studies in South Kensington to get whatever hex/bad vibes somebody had put on me removed.

Back then I didn't know or feel that the Western Church could help me with those situations. Certainly not the Church of England. I knew the Catholic faith took these matters more seriously as many priests are versed in conducting exorcisms and clearing for example. I have two Catholic friends who have really helped me over the years and one, Annette organised for a Catholic priest to come to the flat to pray and clear it. And another friend who has been a rock, Beans I call her. She had come to help me several times over the years to clear my flat with the instructions from Eric. We had to follow his instructions to the letter, no deviating. This involved white candles, a brass incense holder on a chain so that you could disperse the incense throughout the rooms, frankincense and myrrh, holy water, a bible, white handkerchief and a couple of pots and pans! Beans used to be in an all-girl band, the original Spice Girls of the Eighties and had to perform a cleansing previously at the house of a girlfriend of a famous rock star who had died under strange circumstances involving satanic forces. The woman was becoming comatose and mould and mushrooms were growing rampantly in the rooms in her house.

Beans was promptly summoned to my flat as I was too scared and didn't want to do this process by myself, Beans is always there for me and her help is so much appreciated. When I had met Pietro and we were seeing each other and particularly before the wedding as I mentioned everything was going haywire I had gone to see Eric, and he confirmed my suspicions that Janet had put witchcraft on us. I never said much to Eric when I went for a reading.

He would pray and then start talking and using his symbols. I wasn't allowed to talk but only to confirm yes or no to what he was telling me. He was so accurate, it was scary. He is a very unassuming man, however, judges from America and a former American President have consulted him. I can't tell you any more than that. I am not sure how much he will allow me to say about him. He told me I was right that Pietro's ex was putting voodoo on us. He told us that he saw her going to someone to help to put it on us. He described who I took to be Janet. I have never met her, but he said she was a tall, black, good looking woman. He gave me some prayers to counteract what she was doing. And instructions on how to take a lemon bath to protect and cleanse as she was madly jealous and wanted revenge. Great! After leaving the session, once the car door was shut, a phone call was made to Pietro. He was not very happy. It's all very well me going on about my suspicions to him but for someone like Eric to confirm it and to describe the person doing it, who I believed to be Janet, was very upsetting. For me it was total confirmation.

## SUPPORT NETWORK

I told my mother about what Eric had said. She didn't agree with me going to see him but took on board what he had confirmed. My mother had been praying for us at this stage as had Pietro's parents. Although Pietro's parents are Italian, they are Pentecostal and not Catholic. His father, Riccardo is a lay pastor. They started praying hard for us too. So, to be honest we came more to Christianity and to our prayer life because we needed protection. At this point in time we were praying for protection against whatever it was that Janet was doing. We had to have a united front. The other four of my spiritual advisors were all in unison too. None of the four knew each other and lived in different parts of the London or the UK. They all said that Janet was messing with witchcraft and voodoo and trying to affect us. That strengthened my resolve. My mum would say throughout this whole situation that if we were Christians then nothing could harm or touch us.However, she fluctuated in what she thought. Sometimes she could see things were happening that defied rational explanation. And at other times she would dismiss it. She does acknowledge that some family members in India in the past had caused problems and she said an aunt had put a curse on us. She also said as children in India, herself and her brothers would play a game lying under trees in their garden in the evening and push off spirits that would land on them from the trees. That's why many Indian's are wary of walking under trees at night.

I mentioned Riccardo, Pietro's father, would sometimes take the lead at their Pentecostal church in Rome. There was a strong community there and they had good friends in that church. Three of their friends gave us a lot of support, Martina, Arianna and Miriam. Martina in particular was a powerful, prayerful Christian who was prophetic and had visions, she had a sister called Sofia who was also strong in her faith. They were originally from South America and knew what macumba/voodoo entailed as it is widely used or practised in their homeland. She had confirmed what Eric and my four other spiritual advisors had been telling me about where the bad energy was coming from

Pietro would spend part of most nights of the week praying with Martina over the phone for deliverance. I know it was to help us, but I found it a bit too much at times. He would go off to the bedroom and even if the praying was in Italian, it would have been good to have been included now and then. I understood quite a bit of Italian then even if I couldn't speak very much. Pietro could go overboard at times. I felt excluded and I asked him if he would be comfortable with me doing the same with a male friend virtually every night. He would look aghast as if I was accusing him of having an affair when they were only praying. He didn't get it.

I did appreciate Martina praying for us. She would have visions of a big snake or spiders in Pietro's showroom. I could see the snake quite clearly. On our regular trips to Italy, Pietro's parents would call Martina, Arianna and Miriam over to their house for dinner followed by a prayer session for our protection. This was very comforting. During the period that Pietro had moved into his new showroom and selling only the Murano glass bowl in the first three months, I decided to visit Eric again. I wanted to know why Pietro's business was not doing well and exactly what Janet was up to. On three or four occasions, Pietro met with Eric to receive guidance. We were totally fed up. It was beyond me why she was continuing with her malevolence after all this time. Surely, she must be getting bored with it. Eric would tell me what was going on.

A few minutes into the session he confirmed that Janet was still at it and then he started talking about someone else who was putting witchcraft on us! This was surprising. He went onto describe this second person. They were female, had grey/whitish hair, wore glasses, was slim and had a strong accent. I knew who it was straight away from his description, he was so accurate. It was Helga, I was furious. We had had our suspicions about Ken and Helga because of their weird behaviour but to have it confirmed like this was something else.

Once again Eric gave me advice on how to deal with this situation and he prayed for me. Like last time as soon as I got to my car the phone call to Pietro was made. I told him what Eric had said about Janet still putting bad vibes on us and now a second person was doing the same. Then the uncanny description he had given of the person, there was silence on the other end of the phone. Maybe I should have waited and told him when I got back to the showroom. Pietro had a temper on him, and I had the awful feeling he would rush next door and have an altercation with Ken and Helga. After a few moments Pietro spoke, well he was swearing in Italian. Trying to calm the situation it was decided nothing should be done until we both talked about it when I got back to Kings Road.

We talked it over at great length. What could we do? If we confronted them, they could just deny it and say we had lost our senses. "Oh yes, Gita went to have a reading and it came out that you, Helga are putting witchcraft on us. Stop it at once!" Man alive. What is wrong with these people? Why would anyone want to be so evil and wish harm on others?

It was decided that we would do exactly the same as with Janet, keep praying, get help from my advisers, tell our parents the latest news and get them and Martina and company to intensify their prayers for us as we were being targeted from two different sources now. At this stage we were novices to the whole Christian spiritual warfare scene. With all this prayer help the situation in the showroom started to improve and Pietro started selling his furniture and chandeliers. In fact, the business started doing well. This made some of the other dealers envious and led to some friction. We all have those friends who are happy to support you when things are going badly for you but it's a different story when you are doing well.

Let me reassure you if you don't have the courage or strength to remove these people out of your life then thankfully the Creator will remove them for you in His timing. With all this going on we had to keep our prayer life going because it was noticeable to us that the energy would change in three-month cycles. It followed a pattern. The business would do well and then it would flatline. It became exhausting. I always knew what Helga and Ken would be doing with their incense burning and clanging Tibetan bells. I have a set myself somewhere. As an instrument they are beautiful. These things are meant to be used for calm and meditation. It's the intention behind their use that makes all the difference. All the while Ken would come in to Pietro's every morning to say hello, make small talk, purport to be friendly for a few minutes and then go back to his space and come up with ways to upset us. There was a tangible change in the atmosphere. Things felt subdued, lacking energy.

Things were stuck in a cycle, like in the film Groundhog Day. Regular clients and potential clients would not come into Pietro's, they walked past as if they couldn't see the showroom, and items that were previously sold were no longer wanted. Then strange smells, like strong manure would waft into the shop from the common parts. Everyone commented on this. This was familiar to me as this had happened to me a few years earlier in my flat when another lovely person had put a hex on me then. This is a common sign of demonic activity/witchcraft. The first time that had happened to me it was scary, this time I knew what it was, and it was just annoying.

# PASTORAL HELP

Around this time, I went for an audition for a Christian movie. The audition came through a friend of mine, Carol. She is another singer who I met through one of my music producers, Charlie. Carol's half- brother, Pastor D, was making the movie. He is a knowledgeable and powerful man of God. His father had been a well-known Nigerian film maker and theatre producer. I went to the audition; my audition was conducted by him and I got through. This has since led to a strong, lasting friendship with him and his wife RM.

They held regular prayer meetings for the film of which I became an attendee. At one of the first meetings I met another powerful pastor called Pastor B. She is a lovely, strong woman of God. She would take some of the meetings when Pastor D would be travelling around the world to raise money for the film project. She also became my close friend and adviser. It is no exaggeration to say I am still here and standing because of them. They have protected me and kept me sane. They got to hear what was going on in my life and quickly Pietro was invited to attend the meetings too. I knew from the outset they were divinely placed in our lives. They are highly anointed and prophetic.

Both Pastor D and Pastor B immediately received that we were under a massive spiritual attack. They also knew where it was coming from. We became fixtures at the Thursday evening meetings in South London. These meetings were uplifting, and it was so good to have more prayer help on our side especially in the form of such experienced pastors. We were prayed for regularly at the meetings which we really needed and appreciated. Which was a great addition alongside our parents, and Martina and friends. This is when I started to learn about proper spiritual warfare.

Pastor D arranged to come to the showroom and to our flat to see what was happening and what he would receive and perceive while physically present.

When he came in, we made out he was a client to the other dealers, we didn't want them knowing what was going on with us. We had to protect ourselves. He walked around the building saying nothing, just taking everything in.

When we got to Pietro's showroom, he was very deep in thought. After having spent a few minutes there he said we should pray. With the prayers finished he told us he didn't like the atmosphere in the building, he said it was very dark, there was a lot of ill feelings and jealousy. He confirmed that our immediate neighbours were using the powers of darkness against us. He prophesied that there would be a big shaking in the building and for us not to be afraid. That people would be leaving the building but not us. He prayed for our deliverance, protection and blessing. Once the showroom was prayed for and blessed, we took him to the flat and he prayed and blessed that too.

We felt much better and reassured. We felt more secure and able to tackle Ken and Helga's harassment. They continued to get under our skin especially Pietro's and with his Italian temperament he would say he wanted them dead! I remember an occasion when Pietro's website designers had come in to visit us and to check that he was happy with their work and we were all upstairs on the mezzanine talking and Enzo said that Ken was putting things in the way of the common parts again. That was it. Pietro quickly rolled up his shirt sleeves, took off his expensive watch, put it on the table and started to run down the stairs. I was trying to stop him but wasn't fast enough because I was on crutches after injuring my ankle. So, I yelled to Enzo to go after him and stop him from punching Ken. Poor Enzo was desperately holding him back. I told Pietro he was playing right into Ken and Helga's hands because all it would take was for him to hit Ken and then he would be arrested and facing assault charges. If that wasn't bad enough and he was only arrested and not charged that would impede him travelling to the US on business in the future. Pietro was exporting some of his items all over the world by now and was invited to go to one or two countries to expand the business. He was thinking it over but now wasn't the right time especially as all these crazy situations were happening. However, it was something for the future. Currently things were totally unpredictable.

A while after this when there was a prolonged spate of their campaign, we asked Pastor B to come in and pray for the business. Pastor D was away travelling and luckily Pastor B lived only a short distance away from us. I went and picked her up and took her to the showroom after closing time. Once again, we didn't want the others to know what we were doing or to alert them. She came into the building and she posed as a client as had Pastor D. I could see as she was walking through the building, she was concentrating and I knew she was receiving from above. She didn't like the energy in the building either especially in our neighbours' space.

When we got into Pietro's we made ourselves comfortable on the plush sofas to discuss the situation and our needs. Pastor B used her anointing oil in all the corners of the showroom including the mezzanine. We started to pray and when we were by the entrance to Pietro's and the gap in the common parts next to Ken and Helga's entrance she prayed loudly and very forcefully for the invisible barrier there to crumble and fall down. We received more confirmation those vile people had put a spiritual barrier up as we suspected and that's why some people would just walk past as if Pietro's showroom wasn't there, and why the business wasn't doing well and numerous other things. A spiritual barrier can be just as strong as any physical barrier.

She went on to tell us not to put names as to who we thought was putting the witchcraft on us, but to pray for protection and judgement against enemies known and unknown. She told us that it would become clear in a few days who was doing this to us. Something would happen to whoever it was. That would be the proof. And for us to just watch and observe. The other thing was that she would have to come back for the next two nights because this bad energy would take three evenings in a row to clear as whatever had been put on us was very strong. So, the process was repeated for the three nights and there was a definite improvement in the feeling and atmosphere of the showroom after that.

# CHAPTER 5

×)(×

# BACKFIRE

Everything Ken and Helga had wished or put on us would backfire on them. They had wanted us to split up, our health to suffer and for our business to go bust. This all happened to them. They split up and both of their businesses were failing miserably. Her healing business was not going well, she had to give that up. Not surprising because her energy was off. She had to find other work. Helga was a typical opportunist. She didn't care that Ken was married when she met him. She must have seen the showroom and thought he was worth a few quid. What she didn't realise was that most of the furniture was on sale or return from other dealers or suppliers. I am sure he didn't tell her about his debts either. She targeted him and I was convinced she was a wicken of some sort. Whatever she did, it worked on the poor man. As I mentioned he started a relationship with her and treated his wife very badly.

Looking back on my situation there were other elements at play and certain parallels. So, what Helga didn't know in her gold-digging attempt was that Ken was in serious debt. He owed the landlords of the emporium about £88,000 in back rent. They had been very patient. He owed his suppliers a lot of money too. Everyone in the building knew this. Pietro and I had been praying for us to be delivered from him permanently and for him to get thrown out of the building for not paying the rent owed. Helga can't have been happy when she realised he was in such a financial mess. She soon split up with him and she was coming in less and less to help him at work until she stopped altogether. Everyone in the building was happy about that. She must have been too embarrassed about the situation. We had prayed that we wouldn't have to see her anymore either and for both to be removed from our spheres of influence.

Pietro being extremely intuitive had the gift to see things accurately that had either happened in the past or were about to happen. He would sometimes give mini readings to people. I wasn't very keen on him doing this and advised him to be careful.

Pietro was now having visions that Ken's showroom was empty and up for rent. I think the landlords had been nagging Ken to pay them the rent owed for nearly two years. They were being lenient because he had been there a long time. They wouldn't have been so lenient with the other dealers. They had never sent the bailiffs after him in all that time.

After three evenings, Wednesday to Friday, of Pastor B praying in Pietro's showroom and us feeling more positive over that weekend than we had in a long time, there was a surprise in store. On the Monday there was a big commotion on the first floor. The bailiffs had come into Ken's showroom and demanded the £88,000 from him there and then! Pietro and I were speechless. This was the sign that Ken and Helga were truly behind the spiritual attack. This was what our pastor was alluding to. We were so happy that he would be leaving the building at last.

When people have bad or evil intentions towards others, or do awful things, everything has a cause and effect. This is a Universal Law. There will always be divine retribution, karma some may call it. It may not be immediate, but it will always come sure as night follows day. Just as the truth will always come out eventually. God is the silent witness and vengeance is His not ours. Commit these people into His hands. It can be hard, you may want to take matters into your own hands and do things by your own efforts. Believe me I know. Patience is required.  It amazes me that these people think that what they are doing is going unnoticed and that they are getting away with it. To be honest in most cases it does go unnoticed because a lot of people in the Western world are asleep. It is satisfying to know that in my case they picked on the wrong person.

You don't have to convince people that the powers of darkness exist. Entire religions are based on voodoo and Macumba. It is not just black African ministers that rally against these forces. Thank goodness for ministries like Derek Prince Ministries and Gabriel Fernandes. Derek Prince was a white, middle class Eton and Cambridge educated evangelist. White American, evangelical best- selling author, John Eldredge of Walking with God, don't need to be convinced that we are not fighting against flesh and blood but powers and principalities. Christ came to earth to do four things, to preach, teach, heal and cast out demons. This fourth one has been forgotten about in many countries and denominations of churches which means so many people are living in ignorance or disbelief and their lives are in pieces.  There is a movement and there is hope. God is in us and you can fight back and protect yourselves and loved ones. We have the authority.

Our relief was short lived. Somehow Ken had apparently managed to persuade the bailiffs that he would pay them £2000 a week. And some of the other dealers decided to help him because they didn't want an unknown dealer coming into the building and taking his space. It was rumoured that Helga, who had previously sold her small property in Germany had also given him money, £30, 000 to help pay towards some of his debts on the promise that he would pay her back in the near future when his business picked up. We were devastated because we thought we were finally rid of him only to have to deal with him again for heaven knows how long now.

Pastor B calmed us down and said at least we had the revelation as to who was responsible for the bad energy. She said we didn't have to worry about him because God was going to deal with him harshly and that something awful was going to happen to him. Her prophecies are never wrong. We just had to put up with him for the time being.

In the period that Helga was coming in less and less into the building it was easier to talk to Ken. He was more relaxed without her being there. I told him quite boldly on several occasions that he shouldn't listen to her and that I had a feeling she was making him do things he didn't want to do. I also told him to tell her to stop doing what she was doing because it would come back on her and him. He would look at me sheepishly, I was sorry for him and was trying to help him. I was convinced that he was under her influence and spell. Looking back, I am sure that was the case especially when we reflected on certain patterns in his behaviour.

It was only a short while after the bailiffs had come in that Pietro discovered the voodoo dolls in the vase in his showroom. After the initial outrage and having to keep quiet and say nothing to Ken and Helga, which took a huge effort, we felt the energy in the showroom lift. It had been so much better since Pastor B had come in and prayed. Business increased considerably which really annoyed our neighbours. We didn't pay Ken much attention, plus it was much better without Helga coming to the building all the time. The discovery of the dolls was just the biggest confirmation to date that black magic and witchcraft had been put on us.

Before the discovery I had had a nagging feeling that something was still in the showroom. Pietro said, "No it had all gone. Especially after the three days of prayers by our pastor."

I knew that Pastor B's prayers had nullified whatever had been put there to harm us. But it was good to know I hadn't been wrong, and the discovery of the voodoo dolls showed they had been the anchor to all the negativity and chaos previously. I believe things are revealed to us in due season.

Another thing revealed to us during this period, was Bettina, Pietro's mother had been at home gardening in the back garden in Ronciglione when she had dug something up whilst potting plants. It was an effigy. Pietro had mentioned it to me in passing but with everything going on I hadn't paid much attention to it. I thought it was just an ordinary straw type of effigy. Nothing was surprising me by now. Pietro tells me what she had found was also a rat shaped effigy with 'London' written across the front of the T shirt it was wearing!

"What?" I exclaimed.

Why hadn't Bettina told us exactly what she had found before?! He said his mother hadn't said anything until he had described to her the ones he had found in the showroom. I concluded Janet must have put it there on one of her trips to Italy when she was still with Pietro. She had been wanting to marry him and was trying to tie Italy and London together. She knew his parents weren't keen on her. Where were people getting these horrible objects from? Pietro's colleague, Al told us it was easy to buy them and that his son had two in his car attached to his rear-view mirror, where some people usually hang their fluffy dice! He said his son used it as a deterrent as if to say, 'Watch out! Look who you are messing with.' I had been taken aback and told him his son should remove them as he was messing with things he didn't understand. Soon after I had said this, his son was involved in a very bad car crash and was in hospital for a long time.

The funny thing is however much Pietro and Ken would argue, Ken was so thick skinned that he would come into Pietro's most mornings as if nothing had happened. It was so odd. And for a few weeks he hadn't noticed that the vases had been sold and were no longer there and I was sure that he was only coming in to check they were still there. That was odd too. It was as if he couldn't see that they had gone. We were being protected. Something in our favour this time! It was only when Helga came in one day to help Ken with his accounts that it became apparent to them that the vases had gone.

Helga did her usual routine of coming into Pietro's showroom to meditate on his plush sofa that's when she must have noticed that the vases were not there. The next thing I know a few days later Pietro tells me when he went over to his entrance to look out for someone he was expecting, there was Helga trying to take pictures of the front of his shop with her phone camera from the opposite landing. He said he had smiled and posed for her and she quickly put her phone down. He suddenly realised what she was doing and wanted to go over to her and take her phone off her and smash it. As the vases were sold she must of thought that the dolls went with the new owner of the vases and that we hadn't found them. As her precious voodoo dolls had gone, she needed photographs of Pietro's showroom as the new anchor for her witchcraft! She was hell bent on continuing with her wickedness.

This prompted me to see Eric because I wanted to tell him the latest. He wasn't surprised as he had said from the beginning that this woman was doing witchcraft on us and the effigies were irrefutable evidence. He then told me that Helga didn't have the power to do this kind of magic on her own and that she was going to an African woman and was paying her to put voodoo on us just like Janet had done. On leaving Eric's house the neighbours must have heard me cussing all the way down the street until I got to the car. Armed with this bit of information I told Pietro who by now was really wound up especially since Helga was continuing with her efforts. There seemed to be no let up. It was a constant battle. You can't pray once and hope all your problems will be miraculously solved. You must pray and keep on praying as we found out in our situation. Even though our support group was there for us business suddenly flatlined again, same pattern. It's times like this that you do lose heart and faith. Everyone was trying their best but what was happening? Why weren't our prayers being answered?

I had called the College of Psychic Studies a few months earlier to get hold of the woman who had helped me many years ago to remove a hex that was put on me. This woman, Gill had left the College and was operating solo. She was doing very well and was always booked up. I tried to call her, and her answerphone message said she was booked up months in advance and you had to call on a certain date and time for an appointment. I kept trying and it was constantly engaged and then when the line was clear the answerphone message said all the appointments had gone for the next few months.

I called the College back and they recommended that I go to see another woman called Marge. An appointment was made and Pietro and I went. I learnt how to put everyone's names that I thought was putting juju on us on a piece of paper, pour water into ice cube maker, put the paper with the name of each person in a separate ice cube compartment and freeze them. This should freeze what they were doing energetically. I did this but I wasn't entirely comfortable with it and I wasn't sure it would work. Apparently, this is quite common advice in some energy circles.

In the end Pietro said it wasn't very Christian and I removed them from the freezer. I was desperate and wanted to try everything. A few months down the line I thought I would try and get hold of Gill again. Same rigmarole, I had to wait until a certain date and time to call. When I did call, the line was constantly engaged until it became free and the message said all the appointments had gone. On a long shot I left a message for Gill saying I had seen her previously and I needed her help like before. A few days later I got a call back and Gill said she couldn't see me personally as she was fully booked but she would give me a telephone appointment. I was very grateful. The call was arranged and made for when I was at Pietro's.

She said straight away there was darkness and 'a cloak,' around the showroom that was preventing people from seeing it and coming in. She said there was major witchcraft operating. She said now she could see what was happening she would help to remove the energy and cleanse the showroom remotely. I felt I needed everyone that I knew who could help in some way to help. Also, that whatever was being used against us was recurrent despite regular visits and prayers from our pastors. I didn't realise fully that we all have the power and authority to deal with it ourselves and that my having my feet in two camps was not helping matters. My pastors told me not to waiver or be double minded and that I had to make sure help was coming from the right source which is God.

## SUDDEN DEATH

Pietro was dedicated to work, he worked seven days a week. The only breaks he normally took were to Italy. These road trips we really enjoyed. Part work, part holiday. Before I married, I had travelled a great deal. It's a love of mine. Pietro was possessive and he didn't like me to go on holiday without him or to go out on girls' nights out unless it was to the theatre. He introduced me to a couple of women who had been to his showroom who he thought I could become friends with and to be my theatre buddies. We did, Dina and Bal, they are good friends of mine now. My sister, Rena regularly went and still goes on weekends away with her girlfriends to places like Rome, Paris, Amsterdam and their husbands were fine with this however, I could not go. I thought I was ok with that at the time and we were newly married, so I was content enough.

My family have had this glorified time- share for a few weeks in Portugal, Quinta Do Lago since 1997. We all love it there and get to spend quality time there with the family. It is a beautiful place and one of my favourite holidays as it is just total relaxation. We have a week in May, three weeks in August/September and we had 2 weeks in November which we got rid of a couple of years ago as no one was going, and the service charges are sky high. As there are so many of us, we would try and stagger the weeks and fit it around my siblings and their kids school holidays. Our marriage was in March 2009 and I wanted us to go to Portugal together in August with the family. I didn't anticipate a problem.

When the time came Pietro said he couldn't go because of the business. I told him to stop being a workaholic and to come. What I didn't realise that he didn't want me to go either! This was something I loved to do. If he was worried about finances as he was still trying get his own showroom, my parents were happy to support everyone. He didn't come, and I went for a shortened period instead of 3 weeks, I only went for 10 days. He didn't tell me until much later how much me going to Portugal had upset him.

He came for the next four years and enjoyed it once he was there. I said once he was there because it was difficult to get him to leave the business with Ken and Helga's antics. The summer was usually a period where things go quiet in the emporium as everyone goes away on holiday especially Pietro's wealthy clients. They disappear throughout August and September.

About four days before Pietro was due to join us in Portugal, I had a vivid vision. I saw these army angels run into the emporium and go up the staircase, they positioned themselves all along the staircase and then they only went left at the top of the staircase. They continued to station themselves throughout the first showroom belonging to two brothers and then the second showroom, Ken's, through to Pietro's. I knew that something big was going to go down very soon.

Pietro rang me on the Wednesday morning of the day he was meant to be flying out. He said he wasn't coming because of what Ken and Helga had been doing. I hit the roof and told him to get on the plane. A friend of mine, Kay, was going to work in the showroom whilst Pietro was on holiday so she would take care of whatever the issue was. It took a while to convince him.

My mum and myself went to pick Pietro up from the airport. It was clear to see he was agitated. When we got back to the villa and my mum was out of earshot he kicked off. He was ranting about how he wanted to kill both of our neighbours. I listened and told him to calm down and that he had nothing to worry about and I told him about my vision and that God was in charge. He freshened up and came out to the patio and the pool. The warmth and clear skies went to work. It appeared that he was relaxing and enjoying himself and the next few days were normal.

43

While lying by the pool on the Monday morning, he suddenly jumped off the sun lounger and announced he was going to change his flight and go back to the UK early. I told him not to be silly, but he disappeared back inside. At times like this it was best to leave him to it. He re-emerged poolside muttering. I asked him what the problem was. He said that because he had already checked in online, he wasn't able to change his flight and he would have to buy another plane ticket back. As it was the height of season they were now expensive. So, he had to stay. I said it was only another five days before we went back and that he should forget what he thought was going on in the UK and make the most of the rest of the holiday. He reluctantly agreed.

The next day we went with my mum and dad to Forum Algarve to do some shopping. We had stopped for a juice, coffee and cake at our usual café. I had been to the counter and was bringing back a tray of goodies for everyone and as I was walking up to the table, I could see Pietro was on the phone and I heard him exclaim, "What? Ken is dead?!" I almost dropped the tray. We all looked intently at him as he repeated what he had heard Kay tell him on the phone.

"Ken is dead?" he said pacing back and forth. I tried to ask him what had happened but he was too engrossed in getting to the bottom of things. Waiting for Kay to give him the details I sat down at the table in a total spin. I knew something big was going to happen but hadn't expected that.

Apparently, Ken was found dead, slumped over his computer. He was only 69. There was no obvious cause. Pietro put the phone down and we all just looked at each other in disbelief. However, Pastor B obviously had seen it. We knew that he would be removed from our lives sooner or later, we thought from the showroom because of his debts but not permanently off the planet!

We should never gloat at someone else's misfortune even if it is the enemy. We didn't gloat. We were just relieved that we had been delivered. The rest of the holiday passed with us being able to finally relax but still in a daze. Just when we thought nothing else could happen at the Emporium, as we were driving home from the airport a few days later we got another phone call from Kay, this time she told us that the owners of the first showroom and their shop manager had all been arrested and the police had cordoned off the half of the emporium! I liked these guys and they were not putting black magic or witchcraft on us so I don't want to go into what was happening there but like I said it was a big week and Pietro was not meant to be in the UK for when it all went down. Our Creator is big.

# CHAPTER 6

—✕()✕—

# WOLF IN SHEEP'S CLOTHING

For the next six months life was so peaceful. Business was going well. The enormous pressure on us had just melted away. Pietro and I had been united in facing and fighting the spiritual attack on us for over four years. The release was tangible. This, however, was short lived. In April 2014 the feeling changed. I can sense when something is not right. It's hard to describe it. It's as if the energy in my body is fluctuating, trembling, shivering. It's not particularly pleasant and sometimes I get a sense something awful is going to happen. And then the tell-tale signs of the business declining as though someone had pulled a plug. People not wanting items they had previously really wanted or just not showing up to pay for their item. I told Pietro it was happening again. He almost had a meltdown there and then. He kept repeating, "No he is dead, he is dead, he is dead."

It was too much for him. I was very upset but knew it was going to come. All I could do was to explain that the woman, Helga, who was the prime source of the bad vibes and witchcraft was not dead and since she was the one who was behind it all in the first place she was very much alive and must be even more angry because she had not only lost Ken but a major source of her income because of his death. We had been spared six months because she must have been grieving maybe for him but more for her loss of finances. She had lent him a lot of money and was using his pension money to recoup some of it, so I was told, and now she had lost it all because he died with huge debts.

She was not married to him. I don't think he had divorced his wife and in fact his wife had to come back and sort out the mess he had left behind. More salt in the wound because Helga had no rights in this situation and they had split up before he died. Therefore, his wife had to handle all the funeral arrangements and closing the business. Helga certainly wasn't getting her money back. Divine retribution. A week after I had noticed the energy change, things were going to get a whole lot worse if that was possible after what we had just endured for the last few years. I had made the statement that I felt the oppression was on us again, when this Italian woman appeared from nowhere.

In the early days Pietro and I were inseparable. We were at work together, home together and travelled together. I went to work part time to help with the finances once the showroom had been opened for a few months, I would work two to three days a week. He had a friend called Martin who would also help especially when we went abroad on business. My niece and a couple of my friends from work would also come in if Martin wasn't available. Very occasionally Pietro would go on trips to Amsterdam and Brussels with colleagues to art and furniture fairs there.

On one such trip to Amsterdam I was left on my own in charge of the showroom. I was nervous as there was no organised pricing system. Pietro knew how much everything cost but the rest of us didn't. Even though a list was scrawled out for some pieces the rest had to be communicated by phone whenever clients came in asking about certain pieces. If he was doing the driving, he couldn't take the call. I didn't want to lose sales because people may only be in London for a couple of days to buy various items which would then get shipped to wherever they came from. I didn't want to look like I didn't know what I was doing and didn't know the price of things.

However, I did well that weekend, I sold a few pieces and it became a joke that Pietro should leave me in the showroom more often as I seemed to bring good fortune. Things seemed to be working okay except a couple of people who were helping whilst we went abroad started asking for more money which we couldn't afford with the erratic nature of the business. One day Pietro announced he had employed a woman to work in the showroom without discussing it with me. I was very surprised and upset because I helped in the business and we only needed cover when we went to Italy. We had always come up together with who we would have in the showroom to work when we did this. I sent in two of my female work friends to help us previously and my niece. Pietro was a bit miffed with Martin who, although was a friend of his, was asking for more money.

Hence, we arrived at a situation where all of a sudden, a complete stranger is asked to come and work in the showroom that I have never been asked about or met and who has 'usurped' my position. Instead of covering only when we are both going away on the Italian trips, she is given the days I am supposed to be helping in the showroom. It was just strange behaviour and a rerun of the Ken, Sarah and Helga situation. Alarm bells went off. We had a big argument about it, and I told him that he had to tell her to go and that she was not going to be employed by him. I thought that the matter was resolved.

However, a few days after this argument I went to an acting workshop on Shakespeare in Leicester Square. It was exciting because my creative pursuits had been put on hold since I got married and it was time for me to explore and resurrect them. That morning I had agreed with Pietro that I would meet him back home after my workshop and we would go for dinner that evening. The workshop was fantastic, it felt wonderful to be getting back to what I loved, meeting other actors and studying the complexities of Shakespeare's work. It's not my area of expertise.

49

Feeling elated and that this was the start of getting creative again I caught the rush hour tube home. Even being jostled and squashed up against strangers didn't dampen my feelings. Once home I showered, chilled out and then got my clothes ready for going out. I waited for Pietro and I waited. It was unusual that he hadn't called to say he was running late or that he had popped to the pub for a quick drink with his colleagues before coming back home. The usual pattern was for him to get home around 6:15-6:30pm if he didn't go for a drink with his colleagues. Or I would go and meet him at 6:00 pm and we would go to bars and restaurants with colleagues and friends on and around Kings Road. As we had arranged to go to dinner, I was waiting at home thinking he would be back at 6:30 pm for a shower and head out. 7:15 pm came and went.

Time to call his mobile. No answer. Half an hour later he called me. There was all this noise in the background, obviously he was in a pub. I said he should have called and told me so that I could have joined him and gone to dinner from there. He said that the Chelsea Football team were playing so he wasn't at any of the usual pubs. He said he was in Earls Court! This made me sit up. He would have had to walk past our flat to go to a pub in Earls Court. Why didn't he call me or pop in and get me? My antennae prompted me to ask him who he was with. Silence. My heart jumped because I knew I was not going to like the answer.

Then, "Matilde," he replied.

I said, "Matilde who?"

"The new girl," he said.

A thousand thoughts ran across my mind. The new girl, the one who he was meant to get rid of I thought?

"Matilde and who?" I said trying to contain my anger. Thinking he was there with her and some other colleagues.

50

"Oh, just Matilde," he answered.

That was it. I said, "Which pub? I am coming down there now."

My intuition was fired up. I was not happy. He had walked past our flat to go for a drink with another woman knowing I was at home waiting for us to go out to dinner. The walk down to the pub was the fastest I had walked in a very long time. He wasn't in the bottom part of the pub, he was upstairs in the dining section.

Once upstairs, scanning the room, it was very busy, I found my husband sitting at a table with his new employee. The one I hadn't agreed to. He saw me, then my face and he knew what mood I was in. He jumped up and pulled out a chair for me. I looked hard at the woman and tried to be polite. This woman made the hairs on the back of my neck stand up. Straight away she gave me the creeps. They could see I wasn't at all impressed. The woman was pretty, had dark, medium length hair, and Italian. She was dressed in black and looked like she needed a good wash. I wanted to slap her. She sat there smugly with my husband and it looked like she knew something I didn't.

Dinner was very tense, Pietro wanted to get out of there. I was rude and I didn't care. After leaving the pub she went one way and we went another. Pietro had a go at me for being rude in the pub. Big mistake. I let him have it with both barrels.

"You walked past our flat with another woman and didn't call me or invite me when you knew I was waiting for you at home?" by now I was irate and could feel my temper rising.

At which he replies, "The poor girl had no money and couldn't afford a beer?"

I was furious.

He said it had happened on the spur of the moment, she had spent all afternoon sorting out the mess in the showroom on the mezzanine floor and nobody else had ever bothered to do it before. As a thank you he had offered to take her for a quick drink.

He tried to explain that because Chelsea were playing that night all the pubs in the Kings Road area would be full of drunk Chelsea fans, so he decided to go to Earls Court.

I couldn't help but think If it was so innocent, he should have invited me along. I reminded him that he was supposed to have told her she was not going to be working for him. I stormed down the road, back to the flat and got straight on the phone to Pastor B, who at that time had gone to visit her family in Nigeria. I told her what had happened. I was not overreacting as this was so uncharacteristic of Pietro, I needed some guidance and confirmation.

Every fibre in my body was screaming something was wrong. It's unusual for me to take such an instant dislike to someone as much as had with this Matilde. She was a wolf in sheep's clothing. That's what came to my mind. If you saw her butter wouldn't melt in her mouth. I knew that I just had to start talking to Pastor B and she would start spiritually receiving. She picked up something was wrong straightaway. This was alarming because I was thinking she might tell me to settle down and that I was being paranoid. In fact, she started shouting that Pietro had to get rid of this woman immediately. It was not biblical. She kept repeating this. This woman should not to be working for Pietro.

Pastor B had never had this reaction with the two girlfriends I had introduced to Pietro to work in his showroom. I told her that he had employed this woman without even discussing it with me and had just walked past the flat and taken her for a drink when we were meant to be going to dinner. She ordered me to put Pietro on the phone to her. He was reluctant to talk to her this time. Normally he would call her all the time for her to pray to protect his business when Ken and Helga were playing up.

He took the phone and I could hear her really having a go at him to get rid of the girl. It was not biblical, and she didn't like the feeling she was getting about her. He was not happy and complained that the other workers had been unreliable or asked for too much money. Besides this woman was an artist and could paint and restore his items. He was upset and didn't like being told what to do. Eventually we all calmed down and it was decided to give this woman a trial period.

Pastor B told Pietro that I was the wife and I had to oversee things and if I thought something was wrong then she had to go. I capitulated because this woman had skills which would be useful for the business and I thought I could trust my husband. When I spoke to my sister and her husband about this incident, wanting to get my sister's take on it, she said if her hubby, Olly, had done this to her she would have been furious and slapped him and the woman! My brother-in-law said it was very uncharacteristic of Pietro which is exactly what I had thought.

Another thing that gave me cause for concern was that my friend Annette had also told me, in no uncertain terms, that this new employee had to go when I recounted what had happened in a telephone conversation a day or so later. She is very spiritual and has insights too. She became very agitated and started shouting that this woman should not work for Pietro and that I had to tell him that Matilde had to go immediately! I was startled and worried. Her reaction was the same as Pastor B's.

## SUSPICIONS

Matilde had only been working a couple of weeks and I thought I would pop into the shop like I usually did to spend time with Pietro and maybe grab some lunch from the restaurant downstairs that had recently opened. After walking into the shop, I noticed this painting on the wall near the entrance. My mouth dropped open. It was a painting of a woman in the nude, blindfolded with her face to the side contorted in pain. Her arms were strapped down on either side. There was a belt tightly buckled around her breasts, belts around the waist and lastly around her ankles. It was so sad, painful to look at and disturbing. It looked like a self-portrait of Matilde. It was called The Bound Woman. It was quite a shock that Pietro who was a practicing Christian, would have a painting like this in his showroom which was usually so full of beauty and light. It just did not match with the style and vibe of the shop. I asked him what the hell was going on and to take it off the wall.

"Oh, you don't like it because she painted it," he said in a sarcastic tone. I told him clearly, I didn't like it because it was a disturbing, dark painting of a woman in bondage, it did not fit in and it was in a Christian man's showroom. Once again, I asked him to remove it. He said I was overreacting. Not this time. I had the strongest feeling it was binding him. He told me she had painted it when she was 18 and now, she was in her thirties. Why did she choose to put that painting in the showroom of all places? Out of the many paintings she had why that one? Why hadn't she sold it in all those years? I had so many questions brewing in my mind and my female instinct let me know that this woman knew what she was doing. Some of her artwork was very dark when I looked her up. I wanted to know what I was dealing with.

There was another painting which looked very colourful and bright. It was of a woman from the waist down wearing what looked like leggings. I think from my memory there were fish painted on them and as you got to the bottom of the image there was a pair of knickers around the ankles. Other images were of people entangled in sexual poses, lots of phallic elements going on with lips. Not very pleasant or edifying.

What also worried me was when I checked out her Facebook page, on her timeline there was this very contrived picture of her lying face down on a sofa. It looked like she was meant to be asleep except she was holding papers in one hand.

She was wearing what looked like a bandeau top and then nothing on the bottom. Totally nude from the waist down, on her timeline! I am not a prude and have done an 'artistic' shot for a CD cover many years ago myself. I knew she had a small child and thought that this was totally inappropriate. You must be careful what impression you give on social media as this can attract so many crazy people on the internet.

I told Pietro once again I was concerned about this woman working for him. Rather than keeping this to himself he mentioned my comments to Matilde that I had seen this 'strange' (that's what he called it) photo of her on her timeline. He suggested she remove it. I told him it wasn't his place to have repeated anything I had said to him in confidence. This was disloyal. I only wanted him to be aware of it because in my eyes she was not the type of person we would hang around especially as we were trying to practice our faith. That's putting it politely.

The following two weeks were horrendous. Pietro's personality completely changed. I didn't recognise him. His happy go lucky personality and warmth disappeared. Matilde was only meant to be working one day a week and he now was suggesting that she work two. I had an absolute fit and said that was not going to happen.

We took the argument to the showroom downstairs to Pietro's close friend, Terry, and father figure in the UK, the one who had paid for half our wedding reception in Rome. Poor Terry was trying to stay neutral. Another factor which added credence to Matilde working at the showroom was that one of Pietro's Italian colleagues, Stefan, had apparently referred Matilde. She had been doing a bit of work for him and that was how Pietro was introduced to her.

I am sure Stefans' own girlfriend at the time would have told him to get rid of Matilde. I believe this is how this all came about, if I am wrong and that's not how it happened my apologies. It's what Pietro told me. Stefan had a space and Matilde used to pay a nominal amount to use it. However, my ever so considerate husband said as she had no money she could come and do more work at his showroom, she could offset this with charging less for the work she was doing on Pietro's items.

It was clear to see what was going on or what was going to happen. We started arguing about this woman. Not only had Pietro's personality changed, his eyes had changed. I didn't know who was inhabiting his body but there was more than Pietro that was living inside it. My girlfriend, Zaelia, told me she thought it was the spirit of the man who had recently died, Ken. I even called Pietro "Ken" at times and commanded the spirit to come out of him. Pietro would only look at me.

I told him frequently that whatever had been attacking the business before was now gunning for our marriage. We used to pray together all the time to combat Janet, Ken and Helga but now he didn't want to. He came home to me one evening after work, I was sitting in the bedroom and he dropped a bombshell saying that God had given him a message that If he wasn't happy, he could leave the marriage. I froze. If he had come to me and said he wanted to leave the marriage I would have said okay, let's talk about it, have counselling, whatever, but to tell me that God had given him that message? I was totally shocked and bewildered.

"Pietro, God hates divorce what are you talking about? That is definitely not God talking to you," I said.

He then said God had told him that marriage doesn't have to be forever!

I told him we needed to go and see our Pastors and talk to them about this. I was worried that he was losing his marbles and he was hearing things, obviously not from God. It's was like when people kill people because they said God told them to do it. I couldn't take it in. It felt like someone had stuck a knife in my heart.

The next few weeks were hell on earth. Every night Pietro would be scared and desperate because he said something was sitting on his chest trying to strangle him and he couldn't breathe. He couldn't sleep and would wake up gasping for air which obviously woke me up and kept us up. Also, he said that there was a spirit in the flat harassing him which I felt too. He would cry all the time. His friends told me he would start crying in the pub for no apparent reason.

A friend called me and insisted on coming to see me because she felt something was desperately wrong. She is an old friend that I met when I lived in Hong Kong. Nora is very intuitive and has dreams and visions. Even though she lived a couple of hours away in Canterbury she said, "I really have to come and see you."

She came to the flat while Pietro was at work and she told me she had had this vision of herself, Pietro, myself and a swimming pool. I was in the pool with Pietro, Nora was on the side. She was screaming for us to get out of the pool because there was danger. I heard her and I got out of the pool. But Pietro couldn't hear her and then both of us were yelling at him to get out. He stayed in the pool and that was all she could see.

I told Nora all this stuff was happening and whatever I said to Pietro he couldn't seem to hear me. I said the marriage was in trouble and that this creepy woman who had come to work for him was the cause of it. Nora knew about everything that had happened with Ken and Helga and couldn't believe that a spiritual attack was still being inflicted on us. She was one of my friends who always said that Pietro adored me and couldn't understand what was now going on with him. When he came home that night, Nora stayed for dinner and it was almost like old times and the old Pietro.

Suddenly he started to cry, and she was asking him what was wrong. For the first time he was talking about children and that I never wanted them. I was surprised as although he was a few years younger than me he said if kids came along, fine, if not, that was fine too as I was his family. We had married later in life. He had not talked about this with me recently as there could have been options if he really was wanting this. In my previous relationship my partner had three boys who spent a lot of time with us. I am very fond of children but was not really driven to have them myself.

This is a subject that needs to be discussed fully in any relationship and I had believed what Pietro had told me. He opened up that night and I thought we could work things out. My friend thought the same and that we would be okay. I was hoping that would be the case because being Christian divorce is not usually an option. Nora stayed the night, and all seemed calm. I felt better when Nora left in the morning and things were good for a few days.

This didn't last. He then said he needed time and space to think things through and I said I would go and spend a few days with my parents. I went to Birmingham to see them and told mum about Pietro and his erratic behaviour. She thought straight away he was having an affair.

I told her, "Don't be ridiculous he is not like that."

On returning to London I was hoping that the little break would settle things down. Pietro seemed fine and we had been attending our Thursday evening prayer meetings consistently. On the Thursday of that week we were due to go. There had been an argument on the Tuesday before because I wanted to pop into the shop and it was a day that Matilde was working, Pietro told me not to come in because he didn't like me checking in on him.

Red rag to a bull.

I said the whole point of having someone to work for him was to give us more time together and not have him playing footsie with his new employee. I said I was going to come in and throw her out. He said he would call the police, I was shocked. He denied he had ever said this later, but it wasn't the last time he would threaten calling the police against his own wife.

By the Thursday I knew I had to call Pastor D to speak to him before the prayer meeting started about this whole situation. The call was made, and I was expecting to talk to the Pastor on arrival. Instead Pietro, who was very agitated, accosted the Pastor and told him he needed to speak to him and walked off with him to the Pastor's office. I was annoyed as I had wanted to talk to him first. The rest of us went into the main room and talked for a while until they both came in.

"Okay, now my turn," I thought.

But the pastor wanted to start the meeting and said I could talk to him afterwards. Pastor D always has the anointing where even if he has prepared a certain topic it can change to a talk on whatever and wherever God is leading him. It is a gift and it's obvious as he is always spot on. He suddenly started talking about adultery and sinning out of the blue. He had never done this before. I was alarmed and I knew where God was leading him. Pietro was not very happy at all.

The meeting was uncomfortable and when it ended, I had to remind Pastor D that I was the one who had specifically called to talk to him, and I was not going anywhere until I had. We went to his office and I started telling him how Pietro was behaving with his new employee and that he had changed. The Pastor told me that the devil had got its foot in the door and we had to close it. He said the woman was an agent of the devil and had to go but we had to persuade Pietro to do it. He said Pietro may not listen and we had to pray for God to remove her. He then told me to go and get Pietro so he could talk to the both of us. We both sat with the pastor and he was very clear.

However, to my surprise Pietro started talking about it not being the woman that was causing problems apparently it was me. I wasn't cooking for him or looking after him. This was the first I had heard about it. I was completely gobsmacked. Every time I mentioned the woman, he wouldn't address it but would blame me for something. We were getting nowhere except I think

Pastor believed Pietro that I wasn't looking after him.

We left the meeting and we had a huge argument in the car. Why was he lying to the pastor that I wasn't looking after him? Why was I hearing this complaint for the first time? He had never said anything like that to me before. He started ranting and raving that he was not an adulterer and a sinner. He also said he wasn't going to come to the Thursday meetings again as he didn't like being accused of these things. No one had accused him. The pastor was talking about the dangers of adultery and sinning. Why this strong reaction and denial?

We needed help and as Pastor D was travelling with his project quite a bit, I had to talk to Pastor B. She is a counsellor. From the beginning she knew about the nature of Matilde. She said that she was putting spells on Pietro and was highly demonic. By this stage I was having visions of this woman coming at me as half snake and half human. The head and torso were her in human form and the bottom half was a snake. She would slither up to me and be in my face. I visualised cutting her in half with a sword several times. One night I told Pietro about this. He was holding my hand on the sofa and when I told him he let go of my hand. It was if I were the snake! He didn't want to hear it. I insisted that we went to Pastor B together for counselling, which we did but it would get really heated and we would argue.

Once again, he was saying I wasn't looking after him, not cooking and cleaning. We had a cleaner and Pietro loved to cook. It was his choice and I would cook when he didn't. Pastor B maintains until now that she held us up as the ideal couple. At the beginning she, like Pastor D, thought that there was some truth in me not looking after him as I should. This was soon dispelled. We then had our counselling sessions with her separately because we would just argue. It was then the Pastor B started to see through what was going on. I had, in the meantime, tried to take on board that maybe I had to be more "wifey". So, I started to cook more and have dinner on a nicely laid table when he came home from work.

Anyone who knows me knows I am not the domesticated model. However, if my marriage was in trouble, I would make more of an effort.

The response I got was, "Oh it's not you. I can see it in your eyes. You don't want to do this."

I was astonished because I really was trying. There is something wrong with this man. How could he tell it's in my eyes that I didn't want to do it? Everything I tried made no difference. There was something else going on with him.

# CHAPTER 7

## ITALIAN CONFIRMATION

In May or June of 2014, we had planned a trip to Italy on business and it was arranged for Matilde to look after the business. Things were tense as she had only been working a few weeks and Pietro was very strange about me popping into the shop on the days that she was working. He didn't want me to go in. He said he didn't want me arguing with her. I asked why would I do that?

I had tried to be friendly with her and tried to give her advice on where she could get help with social services. She was a single parent. Her previous partner, Salva, with whom she had a daughter, had dumped her upon their arrival in the UK from Italy, whilst she was either pregnant or shortly after their daughter had just been born. He went off with another woman apparently. He was not very forthcoming with money and she was struggling. However, I said to Pietro it was not his job to provide for her. I tried to help where I could and gave her some of my shoes and boots, but her feet were too big for them.

Matilde didn't want to be friendly with me. She was very cold and hardly spoke. It became all too clear later. I asked Pietro what was going on? He would deny that he had any interest in Matilde and often refer to her as a silly girl who was too young.

He said, "Why would I look at anyone else when I'm reading the Bible and praying?" He was so convincing and I was trying to believe him.

We had prepared for the trip and set off for Dover as usual very early in the morning. It usually took 22- 23 hours to get to Bad Aibling in Germany to rest and spend time with friends there. This trip was very different as previously when my friends had been working in the showroom, it was my role to take and make calls and organise things regarding the business as Pietro was doing the driving. This time he wouldn't let me speak to Matilde. He would take calls at the various motorway cafés, but he would walk a few yards away to take the call. This infuriated me. I told him to stop walking away and talk in front of me.

I was not happy, and it was simmering all the way to Germany. We arrived quite late and just had something to eat and spent the night at our usual hotel. Next day we met up with our friends Matteo and Kate and tried to chill out, shopping and having lunch in a few regular haunts. We were having lunch and our friends noticed the tension and then it all came spilling out that this woman had come to work for Pietro and all hell had let loose. I explained that I thought she was putting spells on Pietro as far as I was concerned and that he didn't want me even coming into the showroom when she was there. I was virtually banned from it. I said something was going on between them.

They were shocked. Matteo and Kate said that Pietro would never do anything like that. Pietro had been acting strange for a while but on the following couple of nights he was more relaxed and was being closer, it was a relief. It seemed the distance from whatever influence was being exerted was dissipating. I think on the third night there was a beer festival to which we went. We were having a good time, and something triggered me.

Pietro was always a bit of a flirt and on occasion that would tee me off. He was staring at this young woman on a table next to us. This was too much with all the crap I had to put up with in the last few weeks, so I shouted at him. His friends were surprised as I never had an outburst and especially not in front of them. We argued and I grabbed a fork and threw it into the distance in a temper. He grabbed me and dragged me out of there. He said I could have hurt someone badly. It most likely hit the floor. I didn't hear anyone scream in agony. Not a proud moment.

We were leaving for Italy early the next morning which was just as well because I didn't want to talk to his friends about the night before. The journey continued through Austria and through to Italy. I was feeling very down and felt something ominous was going to happen. I said to Pietro that we were under major negative energy and we should protect ourselves and pull together not away. The calls from Matilde about this and that kept coming from the UK. I thought my girlfriends didn't ring that much when they used to work in the showroom. Pietro would do the walking away from me to have the conversation. This happened once too often for my liking so when Matilde rang about a client, I grabbed the phone and asked her what was happening. I told her to deal with some boxes that were on the mezzanine floor. With that I hung up. Pietro started screaming at me. It was demonic.

He pulled the van over to the side of the road and got out and started yelling and kicking the ground hard. Heaven knows what the other drivers who saw this spectacle as they drove past must have been thinking. He scared me. We didn't speak for a long time. I realised I was dealing with something powerful. By the time we were approaching Rome and his parents I said I didn't want to stay at their house and for him to take me to a local hotel. He looked surprised and told me not to be stupid. I insisted and that started another argument. I was about to jump out of his moving van. He was holding onto me. We got to his parent's house and it was late.

Bettina came out and by this stage I was rambling. She couldn't speak English. She spoke French and as I didn't speak much Italian we used to communicate in a bit of French and Italian. I kept repeating to her, "The devil is really working. The devil is really working." I walked past her and went into the house. I think she was asking Pietro what was going on. I didn't want to be at the house. I felt there was conspiracy going on between Pietro and his mother. I showered and prepared for dinner. His parents always made gorgeous food. So, we ate, and I went to bed expecting Pietro to follow me shortly as it had been a long, emotionally draining day.

I remember waking up suddenly. Pietro wasn't next to me in bed. It was about 3am and I could hear talking downstairs. I went downstairs to find Pietro and Bettina were talking. I went in and sat there just looking at them. His mother turned on me and asked what was the matter with me and did I have a problem with her talking to her son? I said of course she could but not about me. We started arguing. Pietro didn't know what to do as his mother and I had just had the first argument in five years.

There was a something brewing, and I felt Pietro was complaining about me. In fact, I knew he was. I hadn't grasped the extent of what he was doing until later. The energy had changed, and this was something that would become more frequent in the months to come. I told Bettina that the witchcraft was on us more than ever and something very powerful was affecting not just the business now but our marriage. I said that Matilde was causing us to argue. I got very upset and when we went to bed, I was sobbing and kept repeating, "I can't fight this on my own." I felt Pietro was not himself and that he wasn't supporting me in this fight as we had stood together in the past when under such attack. I felt so alone, and trying to convince him that there was something wrong with this whole Matilde situation was draining and frustrating.

He tried his best to comfort me, but he looked tired and confused. It was then I made him promise to take us to Rome the next day to see Martina. I wanted Martina to pray for us and to discern what was happening. Feeling comforted by this I fell asleep. It was decided that his parents and us would make the 60 km trip to see Martina in Rome. Something was compelling me that we should see her as Pietro was not listening to anything that our pastors in the UK were saying especially about Matilde. Pietro had stopped coming to the Thursday prayer meetings by now and he wasn't there for their prayers and protection personally. Nonetheless everyone continued praying for him. We set off, had only just left Ronciglione and were on a narrow, winding road towards Rome when a car came up behind us flashing its lights.

After pulling over the problem became apparent the exhaust pipe was virtually dragging on the ground. Bettina understood and so did I, something was trying to prevent us getting to Martina's. She started praying. She is an anxious woman at the best of times. I said we had to get to a garage to see if they could at least tie it up with something. We found a garage nearby thankfully. They said they would try and do a temporary fix for us because to get relevant car parts would take days.

Nothing was going to stop us getting to Rome. While waiting for the mechanic to do something I was explaining to Bettina about everything that had been happening. All about Helga and the same energy affecting the business again, the woman appearing and causing havoc, Pietro's behaviour and our marriage being affected. She listened and she looked a bit sceptical because Ken had died, she thought it was all over just like Pietro. After everything we had experienced and fought against why would she be sceptical now? It didn't make sense. I told her it was worse than ever now.

After an hour and a half, the car was temporarily fixed, and we resumed the journey to Rome. We got to Martina's flat and all sat out on the terrace whilst dinner was being prepared. Martina's sister, Sophia was there, she is also a powerful Christian woman with prophetic abilities. She was preparing to move back to South America in the next few weeks. It was a lovely, warm evening and it should have been pleasant, but somehow one minute we were talking amicably and next the atmosphere changed, as I said this is something, I would later get accustomed to. Pietro's parents launched a verbal attack on me. It was odd and unexpected. Something got into Riccardo, he said I wasn't born again because he could tell by my eyes and that my pastors were not proper pastors. They were too strict. The African prayers against witchcraft that they gave us from the Mountain of Fire and Miracle Ministries were too strong. Strange, they were good enough to be used to protect us against the attack by Ken and Helga before.

How dare the pastors accuse their son of adultery and sinning. However, neither pastor had. They were just warning against it at that stage. Their son didn't have to listen to them or go back to them. In the middle of this Matilde called and Pietro took the call, he was sitting on a lounger a few feet away and he was talking to her about some furniture. She was restoring it and because Pietro's mother is a very good artist, some advice was being relayed between the three of them down the phone. What I noticed by the way Pietro was talking to her was that his tone was intimate. I told him so after his conversation. I told him that I am not stupid and that he can deny it as much as he wants, but my instincts are never wrong. The conversation between Pietro and Matilde had touched a nerve and I was determined that no one was going to mess with me that evening.

We ate dinner and then it was time for the prayers. We were not even five minutes into the meeting when Martina's sister, Sophia, jumps out of her seat and starts shouting repeatedly, "Voodoo, voodoo." There it was. The confirmation I knew I would get and, in a way, no one present could deny. Pietro's mother started crying. Everyone was unnerved apart from me.

I had to stop myself from saying I told you so. Serious protection prayers went up and some prophesying over us. Martina said, regarding me, that I had a couple of friends that were, "In the shadows." I didn't know who they meant at the time.

On the drive home it was a different story. No one was sceptical now. They would have to believe what the pastors in the UK had been saying all along. I thought we could all unite like before to protect ourselves. It was a quiet journey back, all of us deep in thought and reflection. The next morning, I was so relieved that I wouldn't be fighting this battle on my own. In the garden I rang my close girlfriend, Dawn, while Pietro and his dad went to do a couple of errands in town and his mum was in the kitchen.

It was a long conversation about what had happened and other things which my friend wanted to talk to me about. We had a laugh about a couple of things, and I noticed Pietro's mother looking at me through the patio doors. I thought nothing of it, and she didn't speak English so wouldn't know what we were talking about anyway. When I went inside, she was funny with me. In our communication, in my pigeon French and Italian, she commented that I had been on the phone for a very long time and asked why I had been laughing as the situation between Pietro and myself was very serious. That did not go down well.

I told her I was talking to my friend and I could say what I liked, and I was happy now that the voodoo had been exposed. Pietro's mother is a caring, kind woman, however I felt she was overstepping a line. I know she meant well but the next two hours plus was a conversation about how I should cook for her son, get a proper job, preferably in law, not go to Portugal with my family but stay with him and I should iron his shirts. You can imagine my reaction.

I reminded her that I always looked after her son but ironing his shirts was not something I would do on a regular basis. I would take them to the dry cleaners to do it. She wasn't happy about that, it was a waste of money. As for her comments regarding Portugal, Pietro would always join me and enjoy it so much that at times he didn't want to go home. We were only apart for a few days and I was with family. I couldn't understand why she was misinterpreting my family holiday as some form of abandoning her son. It began to dawn on me that all this was what he must have been complaining about to his mother. He was trying to make out I was being a bad wife. Just as he was to the pastors. My understanding of the situation was becoming clearer. I told her that the new employee was the problem and I was warned about her by everyone and I thought she was casting spells on her son. I said she had appeared on Facebook in that dodgy picture and I did not think she was the type of woman I wanted around my husband. His mother told me to make friends with her. I said I had tried but she was always offish, and that Pietro did not even want me in the showroom on the days she was there. And instead of spending time with me when Matilde was meant to be looking after the shop, he would stay there with her watching Italian movies. In reflection, it is clear what was going on, and I was putting up with the nonsense. My friends and mother said I should have gone into the showroom and just thrown her out. I don't know why I didn't.

On a previous trip to Italy his mother had mentioned she would love to have grandchildren. I didn't pay much attention as she knew my age. We married later in life. Pietro was easy or so he told me if a child came along or not. Well on this trip his mother was going on and on about how she would love a grandchild and that she was desperate for one. Her older son and wife didn't have any children and she was looking to Pietro.

I asked her where she thought grandchildren were going to come from? I now realize she was putting immense pressure on her son. I realised there was something more going on in the background and it centered around Pietro having a child. This made me anxious.

When Pietro and his dad returned, I was in an ambivalent mood. Pietros' mother was displaying typical Italian values, and I understood this, they put their sons on a pedestal and expect the women in their lives to run around them.

I am not a drudge and never will be. It is not my purpose in life to run around cleaning up after a man.

70

It may be a generational thing or an Italian or even an Indian thing. My mother was brought up that way, but things have changed. However, we were spoilt because from an early age we always had home help in the form of my dad's patients who would cook and tidy up for us every day in Birmingham. It is not my thing to run around after a man in that way, never has been and never will be. His mother was always cooking, cleaning and ironing. If that's what she enjoys, great. My time is better spent doing what I enjoy.

I obviously did my bit at home and because he worked seven days a week, he didn't do anything in the flat apart from cooking when he felt like it. He enjoyed it and I would cook when he didn't fancy it or we went out, had takeaways. We had a cleaner. He had never complained before in the previous six years. He was told in no uncertain terms that he knew what I was like before we married and that my previous partners didn't expect me to be a drudge and that I didn't appreciate a lecture on what I should or should not be doing and where I can go or can't go.

The trip back to the UK was tense but better than the trip on the way to Italy because of all the prayers in the group, things felt a bit calmer. After the initial tension of his mother's little chat with me things settled down. One thing had struck me if I had gone to my parents complaining that Pietro was neglecting me and treating me badly maybe they would believe me. However, they would want to hear both sides of the story especially because a marriage was at stake, Pietro's parents had swallowed hook, line and sinker everything he had told them about how I must have been neglecting him. If it were true, they would have a right to be angry. There was no truth in this.

## PERSONALITY CHANGE

We got back to England and once again I hoped that now we knew what we were facing we could unite and tackle it together, like we used to. I hoped I could get him to return to meeting with our pastors, if not to the

Thursday night meetings then at least for one to one support. However, once we were back and in Matilde's sphere of influence things escalated again. We would bicker, he would go walk about and he would complain about everything and anything. He would go out without me something he never did before. Now this woman appears in our lives he is suddenly finding fault with everything in our lives. That is exactly what Pastor B told him. It was obvious what was happening.

As I said Pastor B realised this very quickly, especially as he was cutting down my efforts to resolve things. He was not acting rationally. Before I could ponder too much on this I had to go to Birmingham because my dad was having an operation so that gave us another little break. After a few days I went back and his behaviour was even more bizarre and hurtful. He started saying that he had to get out of the flat and he couldn't stand to be there with me and that's why he worked seven days a week. He didn't want to go to the theatre or concerts with me because he didn't want to spend time with me. The words he said that day cut through to my heart, it was so painful to hear especially because at one point we really did love each other. This was not an ordinary marriage breakdown. If it was, I could have handled that a lot better and I could have walked away a lot sooner. It was a battle against demonic forces and for my husband's soul. The intruder was Matilde, and she was prepared to do whatever it took to separate us. Yet, I do take responsibility for my part, in my desperation to save my marriage and solve the problems between Pietro and I, I opened spiritual doors through Tarot readings, and seeking the assistance from spiritualists all of which compounded our situation. The truth is, you cannot serve two masters.

Pietro would walk out of the flat and stay away for hours. He told me that he was just driving around or sitting in the park. He wouldn't answer his mobile phone. Sometimes when he did, he said he was in a bar however, there was a strange but familiar echo on the line. I had my suspicions as to where he was.

In the meantime, I was still seeking to get him help and suggested for him to go to the GP and have some counselling or that we should go together for marriage guidance counselling. He kept refusing. I had also given Pietro even more space and gone to my sister's house for a few days. My parents were very concerned and said that giving him space was not the way to resolve matters. I was not to go anywhere the next time and to tell Pietro that he would have to go somewhere else and sort himself out. I told him he would be the one going to a friend's or a hotel because I'd had enough. In hindsight my giving him space and leaving the flat gave him the perfect opportunity to see Matilde. Why was I rendered so helpless when I had my suspicions? I was spiritually bound too which made it extremely difficult to help myself. When a person is spiritually bound you can't make the right decisions, everything you do gets confounded, you feel frustrated and helpless.My parents, being in the medical field, tried to help and my mum wrote to him to go and see a GP or a specialist because we were all concerned about his mental health. His parents took umbrage to this advice and I think his mother wrote back to him saying my mother needed a slap for suggesting it and that nothing was wrong with her son! His parents had no idea what was going on in London.

Pietro himself kept repeating he didn't feel well and wasn't himself. So, I didn't know why he wouldn't go to the doctor. Then he would continue to say incredibly hurtful things to me which would reduce me to tears and then he would cry for upsetting me. He kept breaking down emotionally. To say we were both an emotional wreck was an understatement!

One night he broke down so badly and was saying that he had been abandoned as a child, I didn't know what to do. He didn't want me to comfort him. He was inconsolable. He kept saying something was broken. My heart certainly broke to see him in so much pain.

I often spoke to Dawn over this period for advice. She had been involved in social services in the past and was very concerned for my health and my situation. She advised me to go for counselling even if Pietro was unwilling. She felt I was getting battered emotionally whether Pietro was aware of his actions or not. She said from his actions and sense of abandonment he may be suffering from borderline personality disorder. You can imagine how he took that. He continued to refuse to get medical or professional help or understand that he was the target of a concerted spiritual attack.

Pietro said a lot of cruel things during this time, comments and statements which broke my heart and reduced me to tears, yet he never said he didn't love me. I think if I had heard those fatal 5 words, 'I don't love you anymore,' that would have been the end of the relationship for me. I would have packed my bags and thrown in the towel. He never said it. So I continued to hold on to the thought that my marriage could be saved. I knew he loved me. There was one time he tried to say it and straight after retracted it saying that he didn't mean it. He said it would be impossible not to love me. It was as if someone had told him to say it and as if he was in a personal battle.

He was fighting with what he knew was right and what wasn't. He was being pulled apart. Twice he threatened to kill himself. Once with a knife, he was holding a large kitchen knife inches above his chest ready to plunge it into himself. I had to slowly and carefully persuade him to put it down, he threw it across the floor. Another time he threatened to jump off the balcony, I was holding onto him with all my strength, trying to stop him from getting to the balcony door. He denies these incidents and dismisses them even today.

I won't forget them as long as I live.

My girlfriend, Beans, was also very worried as all of this was taking its toll on me. She announced she was coming to see me. When she used to visit it was always a happy time for Pietro and myself, we enjoyed her friendship, we would go for a drink or a meal with her. Beans came into the showroom with me on a day we knew Matilde would be working so that she could attempt to suss out the situation for herself. Her help had been invaluable in the past with various spiritual attacks as I have described. She had also come to help me sort out the mess in the flat. We got in the showroom and Pietro was downstairs and we couldn't see Matilde. Beans had immediately clocked the painting of 'The Bound Woman' on the wall.

I can remember the look she gave me. She started talking to Pietro who seemed a bit agitated. Beans decided she would go up to the mezzanine where Matilde was sitting as quiet as a mouse. Beans started talking to her trying to be friendly and came back down a few minutes later. I couldn't wait to hear what Beans thought of Matilde. Pietro commented that he had to start the process of packing his belongings at the flat and that he was going to live somewhere else. We just looked at him as though he hadn't said anything, we didn't want to get into an argument and asked if he was going to come for a drink with us as usual. He refused.

I felt it was like he couldn't step over the threshold of the showroom because of that awful painting of hers controlling him. There was a bit of an argument, but he still refused to come. So, we promptly left and headed for the pub The Chelsea Ram, around the corner. Once we got there Beans burst into tears and said she didn't recognise the person Pietro had become. She said that his eyes were not his eyes and something else was in his body. I sighed a sigh of relief, she had noticed the difference in Pietro's eyes too. I said I was thankful to the Lord that I was not going mad! She insisted that I call Pastor D immediately and that we should go to see him straight away. We called the Pastor and he agreed to see us as soon as we could get to his offices in South London. On the way she said that the painting Matilde had put in Pietro's' shop was horrible, it shouldn't be there and was obviously influencing him. She too, felt that he couldn't leave the showroom. Beans didn't like the energy coming from Matilde. She also said that Matilde looked very scared when she went upstairs and spoke to her, maybe because Matilde was expecting some form of confrontation. When we got to Pastor D and explained what had happened, he took it in stride. He knew what was affecting Pietro and said we had to pray for God to intervene and leave it in Gods' hands. It was hard for him to do much as Pietro was not coming to the Thursday meetings anymore, but he said he could try to talk to him. By this stage Pastor D was sorting things out for him and his wife to move back to the US. He had a lot on his plate. I was still attending the Thursday evening meetings. I would collect Pastor B as usual and drive us to the meeting. We would always talk about what was going on with Pietro. These meetings would run late and by the time I dropped Pastor B off and arrive home it would be midnight. Sometimes Pietro waited up for me sitting in the dark lounge with all the lights off. The way he looked at me would freak me out. He would ask about the meeting and then start an argument. It was getting too much. He was deliberately trying to make trouble.

One night a colleague from my work, Francis, came to meet me and the plan was to go to The Jam Tree on Kings Road to join Pietro and some of his work colleagues for a drink. It started out pleasantly enough, we all had had a few glasses of wine and decided to go for something to eat at Jaks. Pietro had been a bit distant for a while and it was good to have a night out together.

However, he turned his back to me at the dinner table whilst talking to my friend and it felt like he was ignoring or excluding me. On top of everything else this was really annoying, and I had words with him. He walked off and the next thing I see is he is standing in the section between the restaurant and the bar, when this blonde woman I had never seen before has her arm around his neck and is stroking his face. He has his arm in the small of her back.

I got out of my seat and headed towards him. He could see me coming and moves away from this woman and this woman may not have been aware I was coming over; she had moved by the time I got to him and I had a go at him. He got a mouthful because after weeks of his odd behaviour and his being stand offish here was some strange woman draped all over him. That cut the evening short. I apologised to Francis and we left.

76

We argued all the way home. He said he wasn't going to go out with me again as I had embarrassed him. If that was the case that was fine by me. I was going to Thursday prayer meetings without him and the occasional play or dinner with friends. He on the other hand was going regularly to the pub with his mates and heaven knows where else. He was coming home drunk and he had started to drink heavily a few weeks previously which was unusual for him and very disturbing as he continued to assert that he was a good Christian man.

One day I went to Beans' birthday do in Essex. It started in the afternoon, I took her a bottle of champagne as a present, got there early and came home early. That was the extent of my socialising without him. Hardly painting the town red. The other thing is I drank less and less as I was getting migraines because of stress, hormones and drinking alcohol could trigger them too. I have never been a drinker. Two glasses of prosecco are usually the most I would drink once or twice a week on social occasions. I drink less than that today.

Something else was becoming obvious, Pietro took his phone everywhere with him even to the toilet. He would sometimes be on his computer and I when I walked in, he would close it, quickly. That would drive me nuts, it was so obvious. If you look up on private investigators websites, they give you the clear tell-tale signs for people who are having affairs and the above are the classic signs as well as walking away when taking a phone call. I just wanted proof if he couldn't tell me the truth.

So, I would try and look at his phone for texts from Matilde but I couldn't work the thing and he had done something so I couldn't see his texts. However, one night I managed to get into his computer because he hadn't put a password on it at that stage. We had never needed them before because we had nothing to hide. I felt he was hiding something, and I would find out.

There were emails which I thought you wouldn't send someone who was just an employee, nothing sinister but silly photos e.g. of a friend's dog that he never sent to me. Always kisses on the emails. He stopped sending me those a little while back. One email which seemed innocuous but translated it read, 'I am here, and you are there.' It might seem innocent to the normal person but to me it said a lot. It was about two or three in the morning and I woke him up and asked what the statement meant and why was he sending emails like this to an employee? I was really angry, I wasn't shouting, but he was shouting at me for looking at his emails. I told him if I suspected he was having an affair, as his wife, I could look at what I wanted to! That was a fantastic night. We argued for most of it. He said I was being paranoid, and I had nothing to be jealous about.

Next day he put a password on his computer.

## DELUSIONS AND MANIFESTATIONS

During all this confusion I have already mentioned that Pietro was convinced some force was trying to kill him while he was in bed every night. I would do my best to calm him down. Other times he would talk about the spirit that was now camped out in our flat. When I was away visiting with my parents or sisters' house, we would speak on the phone and he would tell me to be careful about what I said and that he couldn't talk too much or too loud as this spirit was listening and could hear everything.

In hindsight I hope he wasn't taking that woman back to the flat whilst I wasn't there. I noticed a presence when I got back. The unpleasant smells that turned up at the shop were also plaguing us at home. One evening I had to go to my local Equity union branch meeting at the Royal Court Theatre in Sloan Square. On my return I found Pietro cowering on the sofa, he was praying with Martina on the phone from Italy. He immediately stopped praying and told me to go open the bathroom door and look inside. Nervously I went to the bathroom and opened the door, in shock I jumped backwards. It was filled with what looked like smoke and this big cloud came out after me into the small hallway. It had a strong smell of incense. I ran back to the sofa and jumped next to Pietro. This thing sounded like it was sizzling/fizzing and it was trying to form the shape of a person.

I started reciting Psalm 23 and Pietro continued to pray with Martina. After a while it stopped getting bigger but it hung around. Getting some courage from somewhere I ran to open the balcony door and our front door and ran back to the sofa. It started to dissipate. It took quite a while and we were sitting on the sofa in shock for a good amount of time afterwards.

Time to get the flat prayed for, cleared and blessed again.

# CHAPTER 8

---◦( )◦---

# THE ONSLAUGHT

It was getting hard to get out of bed in the mornings. Stuff was coming at me from all sides. I went to see my GP who said I should have counselling. She tried to prescribe antidepressants which I refused. These drugs do give relief to countless numbers of people and have their place. They were not for me and some of them can give you the very side-effects you are taking the medicine for in the first place. I had worked for Pfizer and promoted an antidepressant, but I wasn't going to take medication or have the word depression put on my medical records. I was suffering from anxiety and stress as far as I was concerned. I would have to battle this one out by myself.

Sometimes it felt like a long, lonely journey although I was surrounded by my family, pastors and friends who loved me. Mental health is finally getting the recognition it deserves. It used to be stigmatised or brushed under the carpet. It is so important that the person suffering from mental health issues gets the support and treatment they need. This goes for the families and partners too as everyone involved can feel its effects. It has long been known that illnesses and disease have a root cause in emotional and psychological issues. Treat the mind and the body will follow. My pastors and family to whom I owe a debt of gratitude say it is by God's grace that I have come through this battle because many people would have been institutionalised or committed suicide for less.

Through my GP surgery I went for counselling with a wonderful counsellor, Alex, who also helped me enormously. She said what I was going through was very traumatic by any standards. Betrayal can take a long time to get over. Some people never get over it. Normally I keep my problems to myself and will only discuss them with a couple of close friends. Everyone could see there was something wrong and the bright, bubbly person that I used to be was gone. Quite a lot of that period is a blur but thankfully I had journaled a little bit. Also, my memory is usually pretty efficient, and memories are emerging or getting dragged out of the little compartments they have been buried in!

Things were going around in circles. Pietro's behaviour was worsening, he wouldn't go for help with me or without me. His family were in denial that anything was wrong and if anything, I was at fault for not looking after their boy. He kept saying it was one of my friends who was putting the witchcraft on us. That would make my blood boil as I said we knew who was doing it, it was the usual suspects Janet, Helga and now Matilde. I didn't know any one out of my current friends that would be doing it. I had had so called friends do this to me in the past but no one I could think of now. Pietro latched onto what Martina and her sister, Sophia had said about me having a couple of friends I needed to be careful of who were in the shadows. I dismissed the idea. He would not have it that Matilde was the primary culprit despite what myself and the pastors were insisting. And even after Martina's sister Sophia had said there was voodoo on us.

Before Pietro stopped coming to the Thursday meetings, there would be people who were guest pastors or other members who would pray for everyone and those who would be on Skype. They would start praying strongly against the black magic and witchcraft that was on our marriage and some of them had never met or heard of us before. Over a few weeks

Pietro was too far gone, he wouldn't or couldn't hear or see reason. He remained spiritually blinded and deaf.

One Saturday we were invited to a church celebration where we connected with one of Miriam's friends, Jessy, who lived in London. Pietro's parents told us to go because Jessy was meant to be very anointed. We went and met her, she was a small, South American lady with a warm personality.

We were sitting down at a table enjoying the food that had been prepared. She could only speak Spanish. Pietro could understand most of it. I understood parts and she used gestures and wrote on a bit of paper. She got straight to the point. She confirmed just like the others that we were under witchcraft. She also said that Pietro couldn't see or hear spiritually or make sense of anything. Same words of confirmation from everyone every single time. I don't know what he was expecting her to say. He was not happy, and his eyes were darker and not his. She prayed for us and we gave her a lift to her home nearby.

Jessy said she wanted to come to our flat to pray for us and get rid of whatever was causing havoc in there. It was arranged she would come and stay the night a week later. I was looking forward to this. Suddenly a couple of days before she was due to arrive, Pietro said that Jessy would not be coming. Miriam had advised against it, and thought it was not proper for Jessy to stay the night at the home of a married man. I thought it was absolutely absurd because I was going to be at the flat too. Something didn't feel right, but Pietro was adamant she couldn't come to stay and pray with us throughout the night.

What he didn't count on was me contacting her a day or two later and using Google Translate to communicate with her. I text messaged her. She said that Pietro and Matilde were doing things that were not right in the eyes of God. Pietro totally denied this when I told him what Jessy had said to me. He said nothing was going on with him and his employee. Then I told him that he had made up the excuse about Miriam causing problems regarding

Jessy coming to stay the night because he didn't want her to come and spend time with us as she may see through all the deceit and tell me what was really going on. He had made sure that wouldn't happen.

When I was on one of my trips to Birmingham to give Pietro some space, I had this overwhelming urge to drop everything and just get back a day earlier than I had planned. Something was compelling me to just get back to London. These instincts are getting stronger as I get older and it's best to respect them because there is usually a revelation or discovery of a truth. After dashing down the motorway, I went straight to the showroom without even telling Pietro that I was coming back. The surprise on his face was classic. He said that he was meant to see a client and then after that there was a party at his friend Gareth's house.

It was a beautiful, sunny day and I said, "Great I will come with you to your client and we can go to the party afterwards." I would often go with him to client's houses, so I took it as normal. Looking at him closely he seemed a bit flustered. He said he was going to the loo, took his phone and came back a few minutes later. He then said that there was a change of plan and that he had to drop some chairs at Matilde's place because she had to restore them for a client. I told him that we could go to Matilde's house together. He was insistent that he didn't want me to go with him, he would drop them off and then come back for me and we could go to the party. I told him that since it was such a nice day, and the fact that we hadn't seen each other for a couple of days that it would be nice to hang out. I didn't mind running errands with him, but clearly there was a problem with what I was suggesting. I was adamant. He asked why I had returned from my trip early and then asked if I trusted him or not.

I said I did not trust him and why shouldn't I come and see where Matilde lived? It was getting silly and he kept refusing. Finally, I gave in, I said he could go but that I didn't like it and I will be waiting, and he better come back quickly. She lived all the way out in the East End of London. He delivered the chairs and returned longer than expected but I could tell from his face that he was flustered and unsettled. When I asked him if he was alright, he said the Satnav took him the wrong way and he was stuck in traffic. He knew I was suspicious and onto him.

Everything inside me was screaming, I knew what was going on, yet my pastors were saying I didn't have any concrete proof so I couldn't throw him out. I went to Pastor B to try to decide what I should do. By now she had fully realized that Pietro was spellbound, and he was lying about so many things especially about me not looking after him.

As she is totally against divorce, I felt trapped. She also told me to stop going into Pietro's showroom as by now Matilde had usurped me. I saw direct parallels as to how Ken had treated his wife Sarah with Helga. Pietro was doing the same things to me. I felt that there was something in the emporium that wasn't right. My pastors had told us about it and a couple of my friends felt it too. Pastor B then said even if that woman moved in with Pietro God would never allow it to stand. I was horrified about what she had said that it might be a possibility. I also knew she doesn't say these things without having seen them first. Surely that wouldn't happen.

I was standing on the scripture that what God put together let no man (or woman) put asunder. I soon learnt that my own efforts were not working I would have to let go and let God. This is so hard for someone who likes to be in control. Pastor B said I was prolonging the matter by trying to do things myself.

The summer was upon us and Pietro wanted to do a road trip to Italy. Even though the one we had taken in May didn't go well and it was now July, I presumed we would go together. He had other ideas. He was going to go on his own. I didn't understand it, that would be the first time in 6 years. If I wasn't going then I presumed I would be looking after the showroom. Pietro said because of the tension between us he would ask Martin and Matilde to look after the showroom. I said no way was Matilde going to be working in the showroom. This time I stood my ground.

Before he was due to make the trip, we were invited to Sarita's birthday celebrations. Gareth and Sarita were married. I had met Sarita through Gareth and started to use her beauty salon in Clapham. There were several other people also invited. The evening started well. Pietro and I was getting on well for a change. We were sitting in the garden. We had been talking about all the weird stuff that had been happening in the flat with the others. They knew all about what had gone on with Ken and Helga. Gareth had helped Pietro burn the effigies at the Gasworks.

About 15 minutes after we had been talking about this Pietro uttered, "It's here." Meaning the spirit and energy had found us in Sarita's garden. I smelt strong incense straight after he said it. Sarita liked incense but had not been burning any that evening.

The atmosphere completely changed. Pietro had gone to the kitchen to get a drink. Somehow the conversation turned to Pietro and Matilde. Gareth suddenly said that there was an attraction between Pietro and Matilde! I couldn't understand why he would say something so insensitive to me, Pietro's wife. It felt like someone had stabbed me. He knew it was a sensitive subject and Pietro had been denying this all along.

I questioned him. He tried to back track and said that what he meant was, he found the woman that worked for him attractive, but nothing would ever happen. Too late. I had jumped out of my seat, went straight to the kitchen, found Pietro and asked him what Gareth had meant by his comment. Pietro was angry, he said he couldn't understand why Gareth would say something like that to me. A huge argument ensued. Gareth rushed in trying to calm the situation.

Gareth then told Pietro he didn't have to put up with this and that he should divorce me! Absolutely unbelievable. Pietro then grabbed his wedding ring and threw it off in front of everyone. Sarita couldn't understand what was going on. I was so upset and embarrassed as anyone would be in this circumstance and hurt that Pietro had taken off his wedding ring. Another girlfriend, Julie, was there with her partner, Al, who was also in business with Gareth. Sarita and Julie were trying to calm me down. After a few minutes the boys were scrambling around the floor looking for the wedding ring, once having found it, gave it back to me and promptly took Pietro into the garden. I sat dazed for a few minutes with the girls in the lounge until I thought I better pop to the loo and rinse the tears off my face. Whilst in the toilet, the window was open, and I could suddenly hear everything the guys were talking about in the garden.

They were talking about me. They were asking Pietro what was he going to do about the relationship, and if he was going to leave me to look after the shop whilst he went to Italy. One of them said that I wasn't in the right frame of mind and suggested that Pietro postpone his trip because he was clearly stressed. Another one of the guys offered Pietro their studio flat where he could stay for a while just as long as he promised he wouldn't use it as a love nest. However, he declined the offer. I was numb by then. I was frozen. I gathered myself for a minute and came out of the bathroom. I thought I was just going to get in my car and go home. As I came out Pietro had run in and somehow knew I must have overheard the conversation. I didn't say anything. I just grabbed my bag and headed for the front door. Pietro was pleading with me not to go. He shouted to the boys that I had heard what they were saying. They ran through and said it wasn't as they were saying. Really?

I opened the door and got to my car to drive off and Pietro jumped in next to me apologising for their behaviour. I kept telling him to get out. He wouldn't. The parting shot was Gareth saying maybe we would be better off with people more suited to us! That was the final straw, Pietro couldn't believe his ears. What if I had told his wife something like that? I drove home without saying a word.

When we got home, I changed my clothes and just got into bed and once again I was in bits. Pietro was upset because I was upset. He rang Gareth and asked him why he had said those things. This was another example of people around us acting strangely, even wickedly in certain situations. I knew something was going on as soon as we noticed the energy in the garden and the strong smell. This would happen with family members too, inexplicable behaviour from good people. Even though I knew it was dark forces it did not make it any easier to stomach or stop it from being so painful.

If Pietro snapped back into behaving decently for a little while it soon changed. There was a pattern to this. It was clear he was fighting with it. I told him he was like Jekyll and Hyde. The time came for him to go to Italy on his own. He seemed genuinely sad that I wasn't going with him and he became very affectionate. He kept calling me on the motorway journey to Dover. Martin was meant to be working in the shop whilst he was away. I thought good if that witch wasn't there, I was happy.

On the weekend I was working in my part time job and late afternoon I gave Martin a quick call to check that everything in the shop was okay. He said that it was and that it was a bit quiet. I hit my target and finished early so I thought I would pop in and say hi on my way home because he had sounded bored. I walk into the showroom and there was no sign of Martin but guess who was there? Matilde!

I looked at her, said hello and walked straight out. I got on the phone to Pietro who was driving through France by now and blasted his head off. I told him he was a liar and what was that woman doing in the shop when he had told me she wasn't going to work there while he was away. He said he didn't know and that he had put Martin in charge and maybe she was going to help if Martin was stuck or had to sell one of his cars. He said he would call Martin to see what was going on. Martin called me and apologised saying he had to do something else and had called her to help him out.

88

I asked why he had lied and said he was in the showroom? He said he didn't want to get into trouble with Pietro for taking off to do something else that day. He knew I wasn't buying it. I couldn't understand why he was colluding with Pietro to facilitate his affair. He was a married man too. I was thinking to myself how he would like it if I was encouraging his wife to have an affair. What was driving these people to behave like this? A few minutes later Pietro called back apologising too. He knew I wasn't buying it either.

In a way I was relieved to see Matilde in the showroom because on the run up to this trip Pietro was then saying that Matilde was going on holiday at the same time he was, and he needed someone in the showroom. Alarm bells! He said Martin was going to come in. I suspected he was trying to go away with Matilde for a few days. Pietro had been calling me a lot for the first few days of his trip and then he was calling less and finally said he needed a bit of space and he disappeared for about three days.

When he surfaced, I asked him what was going on with him now, I couldn't keep up or handle the emotional roller coaster. It made me sick to the stomach. It was awful not knowing where he was again. Previously he would only disappear for a few hours but now it was a for few days, and he was out of the country. I think he did spend a few days with Matilde. He denied it, as usual. Once again, I couldn't prove it.

When he came back his mood was up and down, and I had enough of this nonsense. I would try something. Pastor B and I decided to get Pietro to her house for deliverance. She was not a deliverance minister as such. Her husband had been a very good one when he was alive, and Pastor D was away. It was worth a try. Pietro had agreed reluctantly a couple of days beforehand to do it.

On the actual morning of the day in question, he was having second thoughts. We got in the van and got to Pastor B's. He was sweating and hyper. Once inside we sat down and Pastor B started the process, her bible ready.

89

Pietro started to shake and couldn't sit still. He just wanted to get out of there. He said he had unbearable back pain. The pastor saw it for what it was. When there is a spirit inside a person that doesn't belong there of course it is comfortable in that body. It doesn't want to leave without putting up a fight. Deliverance must be avoided at all costs for these entities. I was frightened for Pietro; I hadn't seen him behaving like this before. He couldn't sit still he was squirming.

Pastor B ordered him to go to the bathroom with some anointing oil and to put it on his back, come back in and sit and be quiet. He complied! She continued to pray over him for what seemed ages. He was hating every minute. I wish I had known about these things back then.

Because of his performance when it came to my turn to be prayed over it was cut very short. It wasn't me that needed deliverance, so I wasn't worried. Pietro was just wanting to get out of the house. He almost ran out of there, dragging me with him. He dropped me off at the flat and said he had to go to work. I asked him if he felt better and that we should pray together to seal it. He didn't want to do it. The deliverance won't work if you aren't prepared to walk in it. It was clear that he wasn't going to and whatever was inside him was still there as far as I was concerned.

Back then the pastor told me to pray from the book of Luke 8:26-36, the deliverance of the demon possessed man over Pietro every day. It's where Jesus heals a man who is possessed with many spirits/demons by commanding them to go into a herd of pigs which then go and drown themselves. The man finally becomes free and sits calmly by Jesus's feet.

I was hoping this would help Pietro. No luck. Realising that this attempt at delivering Pietro had not succeeded Pastor B and myself were trying to get hold of Pastor D who is a very experienced deliverance minister.

The failed deliverance was hard to take. Pietro was now becoming comatose again, continually lethargic, sleepy and yawning. These are signs of demonic activity and I knew it was growing more intense. He said he couldn't bear to stay in the flat, it was too small. He kept pacing up and down like a caged animal. I said ok if that was a problem, we could sell it and get something bigger. In his mind, he thought I was going to sell, move and tell him to go. I didn't mean that at all. I was trying to improve the situation by looking for something bigger.

He told Pastor D and RM that I wanted to move and get rid of him! My flat is a decent size, and this was just another excuse. He also kept repeating that I only loved him 50% and he loved me 100%. RM said if he loved me 100% why was he the one that was acting this way? None of it made sense. My close spiritual friend, Zaelia, was saying that she saw Matilde in the supernatural telling Pietro that I didn't love him repeatedly while he was sleeping.

One night very soon after his trip to Italy he came home and said he didn't consider himself married to me and took his wedding ring off. I asked him what that meant and was he being serious? I was once again blindsided. He said he was going to leave and only take one piece of furniture with him. This was really painful, and I had reached my limit.

I told him he could go. In fact, as he was refusing to come to Portugal with me two weeks later in August I suggested he use the time that I would be away to find himself somewhere to live. It would save him money on a hotel or crashing on someone's sofa. The worm had turned. This time it was his turn to be surprised. He could do what he liked. I was done.

Strangely enough whenever I was very firm with him he would come back to his senses. That is all very well in hindsight. He apologised, became loving and settled down. He was back to himself for a few days. The usual pattern. Throughout this ordeal he continued to tell me he didn't feel well and that he didn't feel himself. I continued to try to get him to go to the GP.

We always sent affectionate and intimate texts which showed the undeniable love between us. Because his change in personality had happened at lightning speed, I would remind him of what he wrote to me and he would say I was emotionally blackmailing him.

All I ever wanted was to know what was going on and how we could find a solution. His behaviour and messages were very mixed, constantly. I knew what was causing it and I was trying my best to wake him up or help him regain control of his senses, body, mind and spirit. We all were trying to help him.

In the darkest period I experienced something that still fills me with wonder. I was sitting in bed one afternoon feeling low, I was reading the bible and as I was reading, I saw a drop of moisture like a tear appear on the page. For a change I wasn't crying so it didn't come from me. I looked up at the bedroom ceiling to see if there was a leak starting to drip from upstairs. There was nothing. Then to my astonishment another drop appeared. A damp patch had spread only about an inch and a half wide but was right there on the page in my bible. It was an incredible manifestation but this time I knew it was from God and the Angels. I was awestruck. They looked like real tears dropping from heaven. This gives me goose bumps today.

The arguments about Pietro not seeking help for his drinking, his health, abandonment issues and erratic behaviour came to a head at the beginning of August 2014.

Acting out of character again, he was putting sexist things on Facebook and sharing things from other people which were dubious, at best. One example of this was a woman with very tight trousers at some event which left little to the imagination. I said since he liked them so much maybe I should get a pair in my comment to it, he hit the roof. Also, pics of girls in tiny bikinis. It was very odd because he would also post things about God all the time. I told him it was ridiculous and to stop putting posts about God when he was acting like a letch.

Speaking of Facebook, another argument kicked off because an old friend of mine, Dru, who was in a gang with Lily and myself when the three of us were all medical reps, playfully called the Mojito Gang, (there had been a fourth member called Riku). We had nicknames and mine was Gita The Man Eater. This was because it rhymed with my name. This was used as a joke many years ago and for some reason the three of us met up for dinner for the first time in ages, Dru had put pictures of us on FB with my old nickname saying we had had a great evening.

A few days later Pietro had seen it and was angry that someone had called his wife by that name on FB. I said it was a joke and it was only because it rhymed. He told me to tell Dru to remove the post and retorted I must have had the nickname for a reason. It was completely mad, and he insisted on speaking to Dru about it. Dru told Pietro that there was no basis for it and that I was nothing like that, it rhymed with my name that was all and it was innocent.

What I found galling was this was a week before I was going to Portugal and Pietro was trying to muddy my name and divert attention away from what I was accusing him and his employee of doing. However, he latched onto this like a dog with a bone, he wouldn't let it go for months. That's projection for you.

Pietro was going to the pub with his colleagues and coming back drunk frequently. Intimacy between us was sporadic, he would say he had back pain and used it as an excuse. Other times we were back to normal. I went to the Thursday evening meeting as usual. Sometimes if Pastor D whilst we were waiting for him to finish up the group had a chat amongst ourselves. The topic was usually about Pietro and what the latest instalment of the drama was that had become my life.

It had got to the subject of Matilde's horrible painting of the woman in bondage still being on the wall of his showroom, four months after I had, repeatedly, asked him to remove it. It had dawned on me that I should just

93

have thrown it out a long time ago. When I was talking to the group, RM said we should pray that Pietro should see the light and remove it. After we prayed everyone got really animated because they all received what I already knew about the painting and its purpose being put in the showroom.

Carol had become furious, she said she was going to come into the showroom and take it off the wall and rip it to pieces. She was so angry for me, saying it was satanic and binding. I was surprised at her strong reaction. I don't know why I hadn't asked them to pray about this painting months before. They were hugely upset at what was happening between Pietro and myself. They were very fond of him and felt helpless that we couldn't break the hold of the dark forces. There were things that I could have done but seemed to have been blocked or blinded from acting.

 The next day I was talking to Pietro in the showroom and he was being very nice, affectionate even. I thought I would test the water and mention the painting and say I found it disturbing and it shouldn't be in there. I thought it was affecting his behaviour and for him to please finally get rid of it. He said yes!

I was stunned our prayers the night before had been answered. He took it down there and then and said he would put it in an auction. I didn't see it in the showroom again. I thought we had turned a corner. However, Matilde can't have been happy that the painting was removed just as Helga wasn't happy that the voodoo dolls had been removed from the showroom. She must have doubled her efforts because Pietro's behaviour was all over the place again, a split personality like Gollum and Smeagol of Lord of the Rings.

One night he came back drunk and said I was 'his temptation' which I found alarming and revealing. I was his wife, why should I be his temptation? I asked him if his girlfriend disapproved of him sleeping with his wife. He didn't know what to say.

Another night after another argument he stormed out late at night and said he would go to a hotel. There was no energy left in me to try to stop him or reason with him. It had been emotionally exhausting, and I was worried about my own state of being. He stormed back the next morning complaining he had to spend money to stay in a hotel. He showered, shaved and put some things in the bag and walked out again. He was being a drama queen.

I was half wishing he hadn't come back so soon. He should have stayed away for a few days so I could at least get some sleep, which was a luxury at the time. There was no indication as to when he was going to come back and my departure for Portugal was only three days away. It was hard to carry on as normal, but I decided to ring my close friend and solicitor, Karen and told her to change my Will because if anything happened to me on the flight to Portugal there was no way that my husband, who I suspected was having an affair, was going to get my flat or assets.

It's funny how language changes when you consider yourself part of a couple and when you feel that someone is disrespecting you or betraying you. If the plane was to crash on my way to or from Portugal, then Pietro who would stand to be a major beneficiary would not be getting my flat. This was a normal reaction as far as I was concerned, and my close friends told me to do it before anything else.

Pietro called me the first night he was away and said how sad he was that all this was happening. I reminded him I wasn't the one who had gone away for a break without me for the first time in six years, come back to tell me he didn't consider himself married, took off his wedding ring (this time it had stayed off) say he was moving out and actually packed a bag and left.

He was very emotional. I couldn't keep up with his mood swings. I was having great difficulty trying to keep my feelings and emotions together. As his behaviour was so unpredictable there was nothing to do but to get on with what I had to do. This trip to Portugal was a bit different because it was only my parents and myself that were going to be there the first week, the other family members were joining us for the second and third weeks. My parents were elderly, they couldn't manage on their own and it is usually down to me to drive them around and help with the shopping when we are there. I do this anyway whether anyone else is there or not. This was especially important because I was the only one with them for the first week, I couldn't delegate this task to anyone else.

The morning I was packing and getting ready to leave Pietro suddenly appears! He just walks in as if nothing had happened. He was very gentle. It was hard to understand the switch in behaviour again. I looked at him intensely especially his eyes. They were always an indicator as to who I was communicating with. Him or the entity. They were the gauge.

He said he was sorry, that I was his wife and that he didn't want me to go. He wanted to save our marriage. I didn't know what to say, do or believe. I told him that I wanted that too. It was incredibly hard, but I told him I had to go to Portugal because there was no way I could let my parents down. They would not be able to manage without me on their own over there. However, I suggested he could fly out and join me.

He was holding onto me tightly and I thought we could repair the damage to our marriage. At the time I really believed he would fly out a few days later to join me. As I had already booked the bus, there was no point taking me to the airport. He held me until the bus came.

The bus ride to the airport provided some time for reflection on recent events. I call it reflection but to be honest I didn't know what was going on and what had just happened. The feelings of numbness and being emotionally battered came in equal measure. If I had stayed, I knew I would have had a nervous breakdown. The thought of getting thousands of miles away from the onslaught of the last three months was all that kept me going. It took every ounce of my will not to sob all the way to Gatwick. I didn't want to drown the other passengers on the Easybus. I would have cried me an ocean never mind a river.

# PORTUGAL

As soon as I got off the plane that wonderful heat hit my body. It permeated my soul. It sank deep into my bones. Slowly it revived parts of me that I am sure had withered away and died. I lifted my face to the sky and my feet were rooted to the ground, I visualised the light flooding my body from my head to my toes and all the rubbish inside getting flushed out and into the ground. This is very cathartic and takes no time at all, it is so reviving.

Portugal feels like my second home. There was calm and certainty here where it had been missing in London. My parents had caught an earlier flight from Birmingham and would be waiting at the villa for me. Coming out of Customs and into the arrivals hall I looked for the driver holding the placard with my name on it, booked for me by Four Seasons Fairways. Having located him and quickly taken to the car, luggage loaded, and we set off on the half hour journey to Quinta Do Lago. Just being in a different environment was wonderful, the smells, the colours, the scenery. It was going to be a such a relief to see my parents.

I almost didn't wait for the driver to stop the car, jumping out and running down the stone steps to the villa I rang the bell. The driver would bring my bags down sooner or later. There was never a time when I was so glad to see my Ma and Pa. They didn't say much, just hugs. They only knew a part of what I had been going through. They were shocked to see me looking so wrecked.

I decided to shower first, but Pietro called me, he sounded normal and genuinely happy to speak. We talked for a few minutes and I said we were just going to the restaurant for dinner and I would call him from the Clubhouse. Happiness made an appearance in my life for the first time in what seemed like ages.

I am not one of those people who rely on other people to make them happy. I am a happy person overall. However, the joy had been sucked out of my life in the preceding weeks. If you know what you are dealing with you can have a plan to deal with it. The problem arises when you don't know what you are dealing with or what is going on. It's like standing on shifting sand.

For the first few days Pietro called me a lot and we would have our usual long conversations. I asked when he was flying over. Surprising me, he informed me that he wasn't going to come. I think this was primarily because he had made such a fuss about me going to Portugal and his mother had told me that last time I saw her in Italy that I shouldn't go. After about nine days of me being there I could hear the resentment creep in his voice, I was having a relaxing time and he wasn't because he was working. He then said he was thinking of having a break and going somewhere else, but he wouldn't come to Portugal.

Here we go I thought. Then I noticed that when I spoke to him that there was an echo on the line again and that he was somewhere indoors but not in our flat. It was the same sound as when I spoke to him when I would be at my mother's or sister's homes back when I was giving him the space he had asked for.

He must have thought I was stupid. I was biding my time because even though I could not prove my suspicions and he continued to vehemently deny that he was having an affair with that 'silly girl,' as he called her. I trusted that the truth would always come out. Whatever was blinding him, he must have thought was blinding me! I asked him where he was because I knew he wasn't at home. He lost it and was shouting that I was accusing him again of things he wasn't doing and that he was going to go on holiday somewhere else.

That was enough for me. He was not going to spoil my holiday. I told him if he was going to be like that then not to talk to me. He had made me ill and I was not going to put up with it anymore. We would talk when I got back. I put the phone down. He kept ringing me back and I didn't answer again that evening. I called Pastor B and told her what had happened, and she told me that this was too much and maybe it was better to wait until I got back to the UK to talk to him. She told me to try to enjoy my holiday. She said he would push me over the edge if this continued. I emailed him the next day and told him about a Joyce Meyer book I had been reading, that had a section in it which related to a story that was similar to what was happening with us. I said I needed time to recover from everything and that this time I needed space and we would talk when I got back. He sent me a rude email back and I decided to keep to my position of wanting space and not communicating as he had asked me to do whilst he was on the last part of his trip to Italy. He should have extended me the same courtesy.

My parents were very upset with what was going on, initially my mum like the pastors thought I had not been looking after Pietro but quickly saw through the smoke screen. As I mentioned, on my first trip to Birmingham to give him space and time to think, my mum had said, categorically, that he was having an affair. This was text book behaviour and one of their friends had done the same before he left his wife for another woman. She, like any mother was very worried about my health and told me to try to relax and make the most of the holiday and to sort things out when I got back. They said they wanted a meeting in London with both of us when we got back.

I was waiting to hear from God while I was away and could spent some quiet time in prayer. Sometimes I can see and hear things, as I previously mentioned. There was nothing. It felt like I had been spiritually abandoned. Why was I having to go through all of this?

I was lying on a lilo in the pool at the villa one afternoon and I clearly heard the words, "Do not be afraid." It was so good to receive something, anything. I wasn't alone. Then the thoughts creep in. I was wondering if there was more coming that I should be afraid of? It couldn't get worse surely. Well at least I heard something. A couple of days later while I was in the pool again, I received quite clearly, "Stay strong."

Confirmation that more trouble would be coming my way as I had to be strong! Can't there be some good news, I thought to myself. Something like, 'Don't worry your husband will break free and the enemy will disappear?'

Throughout the holiday Pastor B had been in touch, encouraging me to keep my spirits up and to have faith. One day she called with news, Pietro had turned up at the Thursday night prayer meeting! As I had refused to talk to him, he was wanting to find out what was going on with me as he knew I would be talking with my pastors. Bear in mind, this was the first time he had attended the meeting in three months, since Pastor D had given that session about the dangers and consequences of sinning and adultery. This was big news. He had sat through the meeting and Pastor D was happy to see him back there. At the end he said he would give Pastor B a lift home as we always did when we went together. Pastor D said that he would take her, but Pietro insisted. Once in the van Pastor B said he started talking, talking and talking.

"What did he want?" I asked her.

Just as I thought, he wanted to know what I was doing and why I wasn't speaking to him. Pastor B was very clear, she said that his behaviour had nearly given me a breakdown and that I needed to rest, that he should never have employed Matilde and that she should be fired immediately and that she was demonic. That's all she said because apparently, he was driving her all over London ranting!

He said I was ignoring him and that he was going to leave the flat. At this stage she told him categorically not to leave the flat and to wait until I got back from Portugal. She told him if he left, he would regret it for the rest of his life. She was talking prophetically. Pastor B never uses her words lightly in these situations. He was saying the woman wasn't the problem, nothing was going on and he wouldn't regret anything. Once again, her words were lost on him.

I wasn't sure what to make of his visit to the Thursday meeting or his chat with Pastor B. When he had come to me on the morning of my departure for Portugal, he had been all lovey dovey, I actually thought we had a chance of patching things up. Now we were not talking, and I had asked him for some space, which he should have respected. Here he was threatening to leave me, and we were back to square one. I tried to relax and forget about my woes for the remainder of the holiday. I understood and tried to implement what the Creator had said to me, "Don't be afraid and to stay strong." It wasn't easy as I didn't know what lay ahead.

# CHAPTER 9

———— )( )( ————

# THEN THERE WAS ONE

I flew back to London; my parents flew to Birmingham. They really felt for me. I think they wished they could have come back to London with me. They knew I needed support and that I was still very delicate from all that had happened and the continued emotional instability I had been experiencing from Pietro. The holiday had been tense after the first few days with Pietro's volatile behaviour and me having to set boundaries.

With trepidation I walked to the flat not knowing what to expect. Once I got to the door of the flat, I opened it and walked in. There it was. It looked emptier and there were a couple of clothes hangers on the floor. He had moved out…. He had taken most of his personal things. True to his word he had only taken one piece of furniture. It was a very large calf or pony skin pouffe. He had left everything else, all the Italian 20th century design pieces of furniture, Murano glass standing lamp and chandelier behind for me to keep.

It was obvious he had left in a hurry and it felt like he had only left that day or the day before. He didn't even message me to say he was leaving. It was a big shock and it felt like someone had kicked me in the stomach, I was completely winded. I sat on the sofa and cried. It seemed like hours before I could even move. I think I rang my mum. I don't know as it was a complete fog. My bags were left in the middle of the floor and I just went to bed and stayed there.

I know I had been told to be strong but there is nothing worse than emotional pain. We have all felt it. This wasn't the first time either and it doesn't get easier. It feels like someone has cut off your arms and legs. There is that time in the early morning around 3:30 am where you just wake up night after night in pain. Then the realisation that the person you have shared your life with and slept in the same bed with for years isn't there anymore.

The next few days were just a constant circle of sleeping, crying, not eating and people calling to see if I was okay. My parents were calling. The pastors were calling. My friends were calling. They couldn't believe what he had done. My bags remained on the floor. I literally can't remember when I went back to work. I know I did sometime. It's hard to dig this bit out of its box too.

It was about a week later that I finally made the call to Pietro to ask him what was happening. He had the gall to say that he was shocked that I had taken so long to to call him, and how could I do that to him. He demanded to know where I was. I was completely stunned, he had left me without a word and somehow, I was mistreating him? I really felt he had lost the plot at this point. This is the height of emotional abuse. When you've been abused emotionally and then the abuser blames you. It was all about him, as usual. I asked him where he had gone. He said he was staying with Martin and his wife. He suggested we meet up to talk and a date was agreed.

He picked me up from the flat and headed to a quiet pub on Kings Road. As we were walking, he got a phone call from Martin. It seemed like a normal conversation but then Martin was asking him about some arrangements for the next day.

This set off my radar again. When Pietro finished the conversation, I asked him why Martin would ask him about arrangements for the next day when he was meant to be staying with Martin himself and would be seeing him later that evening after our meeting? He fudged over that and I kept it filed in my brain.

We tried to talk; we were both upset. It was the usual argument and blame game. It was not at all productive. I got the feeling he didn't really want it to be. However, he said we should see how separation would work for us and take it from there. He suggested we try to work things out if we could. He commented that the marriage was in God's hands. He was still talking about God.

My mum had got annoyed with us and asked us both to write to her to explain what was going on between us. This was a marriage and she needed to understand. I wrote her an email which outlined exactly what I thought was going on. I think it needs to be printed and framed, everything in it was exactly as I thought. Pietro wrote what he thought his version of events were. It was more of a rant.

We met again a couple more times and just ended up arguing. Pietro told me that he had informed Matilde not to come to showroom for a while as we were trying to sort out our marriage and that she had been upset. Poor thing, I thought sarcastically. I just wanted to get my hands on her at this stage and strangle her. Not very Christian but that's how I felt. I continued to see her in her half snake form in my visions. She was evil, I knew it, my pastors knew it and all my other spiritual advisors knew it. The only person who couldn't see it was Pietro.

When faced with this situation you can pray for the destruction of principalities and powers and the gloves are off. They are trying to destroy you, so you need to know how to protect yourself and loved ones. Anyone who is putting witchcraft, black magic or voodoo on you needs to be dealt with harshly. You can pray for your Goliath's and Hamman's plaguing your life to be destroyed. This is not an ordinary case for forgiveness! Well at least for now he said she was out of the picture. Why was I having trouble believing him?

My parents called Pietro for a meeting. They arranged to come to London and meet him at the flat without me being there. My parents don't mince their words. My mother asked him directly what was going on with him and Matilde. She asked him why he asked Matilde out for a drink and that I had been upset by this. He said nothing was going on between them, there was no affair and that the poor girl couldn't afford a beer. After the meeting my parents told me he had been critical of me, trying to say I hadn't been looking after him and that his feelings for me had changed. He tells one person one thing and another person something else.

My parents may have been wanting to spare my feelings, but I would rather know the truth so that I can let it sink in and get on with my life. They told him that we should go to counselling, which is something he had resisted all along. This time he said that counselling was a possibility. I thought that was a bit of progress and we should try it because my pastors reinforced divorce was not a Christian option. At this point I still had no concrete proof of an affair, only his continual denials.

Pietro was now refusing to tell me where he was living. He said he was at Martin's house, but I had no proof of that and great suspicion that he was not. One morning I called him early and had a bit of a row about why he wouldn't give me the address. He was annoyed that I didn't believe him, he started calling out for Martin and Martin came to the phone! He was very grumpy because he had just been woken up. That placated me temporarily, plus he was telling me that leaving me felt like someone had cut off his limbs too.

In the past we had been to Martin's for dinner and a couple outings near him and his wife's place. It was near Kingston, it had been a while since I had been there and because it was quite a distance away I couldn't remember exactly where he lived. I asked Pietro for the address. He kept refusing to give it to me which made me more suspicious and angrier. It was a simple request. He knew where I was so why shouldn't I know where he was? I wrote a detailed letter to his parents about his behaviour, his moving out and his refusal to tell me where he was. They did not reply. I also found that very strange. I was still Pietro's wife. They were meant to be devout Christians so why were they ignoring me?

In this period, I found out through Pastor D that Pietro had discovered that I had written a Will and that he wasn't in it. This surprised me as I couldn't understand how he could have got this information. I racked my brains and realised he must have looked at my computer when I was in Portugal. I hadn't password protected my computer like he had! After all the fuss he had made about me looking at his computer, he had done the same to me! Obviously, I would have changed my Will if things had improved after my trip to Portugal, but they hadn't, and he had left. At the time he must have taken that as a sign that the marriage was in trouble just as Pastor D said. However, I felt justified as he had already taken his ring off weeks prior, told me he was moving out, and had left the flat.

I received a letter which was sent by registered post from Pietro. I was surprised and its contents surprised me even more. It was obvious he had had help to write it. It was accusing me of things I hadn't done. He wrote that I had been acting unreasonably, drinking, being abusive and shouting at him. He had used the episode of when Francis and myself had gone out with him and I had supposedly embarrassed him because I was jealous when he was talking to my friend. Then supposedly shouting at him when he was talking to the blonde woman at the bar. Francis would later give a statement that this wasn't the case and that I hadn't done that. Francis stated that she certainly had not witnessed any drama as he was making out.

He stated I was going out and drinking all the time. For this he used an example of my taking a bottle of champagne with me to my friend's birthday party, it was her present. He was grasping at straws. It had legal flavourings. I knew straightaway what was going down. It was a setup, obviously he was concocting a case against me. Still I asked him what the letter was all about and why it was full of blatant lies. I reminded him that we were supposed to be on a trial separation whilst trying to work things out and he comes up with this? I also knew that patience was a virtue.

Arrangements were now being made for us to see a counsellor. I said we should go to our surgery and ask his or my GP for a recommendation. He didn't want to go there. There was a reason for this, before I went to Portugal and him threatening to kill himself, I kept insisting he go to his GP, Dr. Richards. He had consistently refused to until one day he suddenly changed his tune and agreed he would go. He went to see Dr. Richards and came home clutching a prescription for antidepressants. He said his doctor said he needed to take them for having to put up with my behaviour.

My behaviour! It appeared his doctor was commenting on my mental state without having seen me. I needed clarification on this. Pietro also said he had no intention of taking antidepressants. I asked why did he agree to having a prescription for them? I told him to stop being so dramatic and that my GP had told me to take antidepressants too but I had refused them and didn't need a prescription to bring back to wave in his face and say my mother would beat him for causing me so much anguish.

It was crazy. His mother was upset at my parents suggesting he needed medical help when we were worried about him having a breakdown of some sort. This was perfectly reasonable given the circumstances. Now that I was back from Portugal, I had made up my mind to see his GP when I got back to the UK. Firstly, for making comments about my mental state to my husband without seeing me, to discover if this was even true. Also, I now had the email response Pietro gave to my mother after she had asked myself and Pietro to write to her explaining what was going on between us. His email had caused even more concern. She encouraged me to see Dr. Richards as well.

An appointment was made to see Dr. Richards, I invited Pietro to come with me if he wished to, but he refused. Once in Dr Richards's room I explained why I was there and that I was annoyed that he had made comments to Pietro about my so-called mental condition when he hadn't even seen me. He said he hadn't made such a claim, and he may have sympathised on hearing from Pietro about how I was treating him but that was all. It was the same stories he had been telling his parents. Anyone would sympathise I suppose if they are hearing someone's one sided version of events.

I then showed him a printout of Pietro's email to me and within seconds the penny drops. Dr. Richards apologised. He didn't realize the situation and how Pietro manipulated it. He needed to see Pietro as soon as possible. I told him he wouldn't listen to me. Dr Richards said he would call him and ask us to come in together. I told him that he would not come in with me but may come on his own.

With that I left and called Pietro and told him what Dr. Richards had said and that there was nothing wrong with me. I reiterated what Dr. Richards said to me and reinforced that there was nothing mentally wrong with me. I told him Dr. Richards would be calling him because he wanted to see him. He said he wouldn't go. Dr. Richards later rang me and informed me that Pietro wasn't responding.

There was no way he would go to our surgery to source a good marriage guidance counsellor. Our pastors' efforts on him had failed. So, we both decided to look for a marriage/relationship counsellor.

After quite a bit of research I found an Italian counsellor who was also a doctor. I thought he would be more comfortable with someone who could speak Italian. I chose a doctor because I thought an 'normal' counsellor would not be able to treat what I thought could be a borderline personality disorder. There was definite resistance from Pietro especially when he found out this was a qualified psychologist rather than a normal counsellor. He said I was trying to prove that he was mentally ill.

I just wanted him to get help. We went to see Dr. Luigi several times. This man was more in need of treatment than Pietro! Completely mad. He would say nothing, I mean nothing. He would just stare at us. We were paying him for that? I would get cross and ask why aren't you going through conflict resolution with us.

He could see that we couldn't stop arguing between us. Pietro would deliberately cause arguments. It was brutal. Every time I said the problems started when his employee, Matilde had come on the scene Pietro would ignore it or change the subject. Dr Luigi recommended we needed to see him for about two years for our problems to be resolved. I had a job persuading Pietro to go the few times that we did. That was my last shot at counselling. We had picked the wrong guy and Pietro wasn't going to go to anyone else. We started counselling in November 2014 for only six weeks.

I still didn't know where Pietro was living. He would come to the flat and we would catch a tube to our sessions. I hadn't seen him for a little while, but it was visible that Pietro was not himself. He used to be very smart and now he looked scruffy, he had grown a beard and he was smoking! He used to chain smoke previously.

I was worried for his health because he had given up smoking before we married. I didn't recognise who this man was. He had an animal like quality about him that I can't describe. He used to walk around confidently before. I used to say he was a peacock. And now he was sloping around. It was weird. I felt I had to help him and whatever was inhabiting his body had to come out eventually.

As we were having counselling, I thought the marriage wasn't over and that there would be divine intervention. During the time Pietro didn't come back to the Thursday meetings though he was occasionally in touch with Pastor D by phone. Pastor D was packing up in a rush to move to the US after Christmas. I was really hoping that Pietro would go to him for deliverance as he is very experienced in this.

I had agreed to see Pastor D before he moved to America because he wanted to pray for me. We also agreed I had to get rid of some items from my flat like books, statues and carvings of Buddha which I had refused to get rid of previously. He said I couldn't be double minded, and I had to stick with God alone. I took them to him for him to destroy. He felt what was happening to me was part of God's chastisement of me for having my feet in the two camps and that this had caused a crack in the door for the enemy to get in. He wanted to make sure the door was firmly closed before he went away.

I have since come to understand that you cannot have your feet in two camps, or two worlds as it were. It's a very dangerous predicament. I had to take responsibility for my part in this whole fiasco and do what I could to rectify and make it good before God.

*Ye cannot drink the cup of the Lord, and the cup of devils: ye cannot be partakers of the Lord's table, and of the table of devils.*

**Corinthians 10:21**

I wasn't sure what was going to happen for Christmas. My parents, my older sister's family and my younger brother's family had all planned to go to India for a few weeks over the Christmas and the New Year period. This had been planned many months before. I have been a very regular visitor to India, but my sister and brother hadn't been for 30 years and their children had never been.

This was a big trip and I had wanted to go with Pietro too. As things were rocky, he wasn't going to go. There was a question mark about whether I would be staying with him in the UK or going to Italy especially since we were having counselling. He then dropped the bombshell that he was going to Italy alone to visit his family for the Christmas season. He had no remorse, and I felt it was a replay of how he handled notifying me of his last trip in July.

Pietro's decision decided it for me. I would join my family for Christmas in Hyderabad before flying to Goa. They had been travelling in North India and I would catch them for the Goa leg of the trip. I booked my flight. There wasn't much point talking to Pietro.

I was at the airport when he called me. He claimed I was leaving him when we should be talking it out. It was impossible to figure him out. He made it clear he was going to Italy for Christmas, and that he wasn't going to take me. Yet now I had decided to spend Christmas with my family so that I wasn't alone during the season festivities, he was emotionally blackmailing me. He was being cruel. He messaged me a few times during my trip to India and accused me of not responding to his WhatsApp message quick enough. He would send me messages saying that it was a strange moment for us and that we were in God's hands. I didn't know what to make of it all, this just added to the emotional turmoil I felt regarding holding onto our marriage.

When we spoke on Christmas eve, I felt incredibly sad, this was our first Christmas apart. As always it is better to be in a different environment when going through emotional stuff and I was so fortunate to be thousands of miles away in the sunshine. The only downside was I quickly became ill. I caught a terrible bug from the airplane. By the time we got to Goa it erupted. This clung onto me for the entire trip and something else jumped in.

Towards the end of the holiday I started to get serious stomach cramps and started to bleed. This was a worry because a few years earlier I had to hospitalised for months with gynae problems. I had ignored the warning signs and ended up with peritonitis and if I hadn't been admitted to hospital when I was, I would have been dead within two days. Not wanting to spoil the last few days or worry my parents I decided to keep quiet until I got back to the UK. Once again, my parents flew to Birmingham while I flew back to London.

Common sense prevailed. I went to see my GP for an urgent appointment. She examined me and said she would put me forward as an urgent case and she was worried about it being cancerous. She said I would be seen within two weeks. I had given up my private health insurance previously and two weeks seemed too long. On getting home I called my parents who told me to get to Birmingham immediately. On reaching Birmingham I was whisked to Dr. M's surgery who then referred me to a private gynaecologist the next day, who took scans and an ultrasound. There was a growth which needed investigating straightaway.

It was decided that it was best for me to go back to London to be seen at Chelsea and Westminster hospital where they had my history and previous treatment. I called Pietro to tell him I was not well, and they were doing tests. He cried hard when I told him and asked why I hadn't told him sooner. He kept repeating that he was a 'shit man.' That was as near to an admission of guilt as I was going to get.

I ended up crying trying to console him. This man was suffering. He said he would come with me to my hospital appointments and any procedures. I got back to London and I thought maybe he would move back in to take care of me as I wasn't sure if it was cancer or not. In the end I didn't ask, and he didn't come to stay. I knew something was preventing him. I also knew I had a small window of opportunity to get to the bottom of my situation.

The GP was given the gynaecologists findings and scans. I was going to be seen within days for my procedure. It was early February and I hadn't seen Pietro since December at our last counselling session. He took me to the hospital and while we were in the waiting room I had a chance to speak to him. I wanted to get clarity. Where was his heart and what was he thinking especially after all the messages he had sent alluding that this was only a dark moment in our lives and God would help us.

As I still didn't know his address, I looked him in the eyes and asked him for it. He still wouldn't tell me. Because of this I told him straight, that Pastor

B had told me he was having an affair with Matilde. He denied it again and got very defensive.

I couldn't push the matter as he was saved by the bell and I was called in for my procedure. It was gruesome. I had opted for a local anaesthetic, big mistake. The procedure took longer than expected as the growth was larger than the scan revealed, and the local anaesthetic wore off three quarters of the way in. The consultant said they could stop, and I could come back and have a general anaesthetic. Biting the bullet, I told them just to get it out as I couldn't face coming back.

By the time it was over I was taken back to the recovery room where Pietro was waiting. The pain was intense, I was doubled over and looking green. He was very worried and upset that I was in that much pain. Eventually he got me back to the car and before we got seated he grabbed me crying and held me so close and that set me off again.

We got back to the flat and Martin came to meet us there because my car MOT and insurance were a due when I got back from India, but I had been too ill to deal with it, so Pietro got Martin to help. Martin quietly handed over my MOT certificate and looked a bit uncomfortable, he could see we were emotional. Pietro was going to give my keys back and I said it was okay to hang onto them. I remember they looked awkwardly at each other. Pietro stayed for a while and had to go back to work.

A part of me won't forget that day, there I was at home from hospital, not knowing whether it was cancer or not, and he just left me alone. I tried to forgive him for that time and just when I think I have forgiven, and I am willing to forgive then a twinge of something comes up. There were other friends who could have come and been there for me but didn't because they assumed he would be there. I knew the old Pietro would have been there for me but this was not the Pietro I knew.

# INTERVENTION

Literally a few hours after he had left me alone in the flat another of my wonderful girlfriends, Ali, called me to see how I was and she was not impressed with Pietro's behaviour throughout the last few months and when she heard he hadn't stayed with me during this time she blew her top. She had just finished working for a very wealthy Ukrainian family and had applied for another job. She said she was coming over to look after me and find out what was going on because she couldn't stand the limbo in which I was living, and we would find out once and for all what Pietro was up to.

This was so good to hear. She would help me somehow get to the truth and I knew I was running out of time to thwart the plans of the crafty. I was pondering what to do, when suddenly I heard God speak to my heart, 'Follow him and you will find out something.' Ali arrived within two days. We would find out where Pietro was living and what was going on with him and Matilde. No more speculation.

We decided that somehow I had to find out or remember where Martin lived so we could check if Pietro really was staying there. She drove me to the area to see if I could find familiar landmarks and then find the house to see if Pietro's van was there. After the first night we realised that was pointless. We started trying to look up Martin's name on 192 Directory. In the end I spoke to Beans who had connections to private investigators to help me. In the meantime, I had looked up some agencies and the blurb on some of the websites was fascinating.

They would advertise their services to husbands and wives who suspected their spouses were having an affair. They listed the classic signs or indicators, such as the spouse walking away when taking phone calls from their suspected lover, taking their phone everywhere with them and also putting passwords on their devices, and closing the computer quickly when the person comes into the room. Everything Pietro had been doing.

One of Bean's connections found Martin's address for us. Ali did the driving because I wasn't well enough and we headed straight for Martin's house late at night, so as to make sure that Pietro's van would have to be there. We did this for a few nights in the first week and Pietro's van was never there. Obviously, we checked a few of the adjacent streets to make sure but there was parking near to the house.

All I wanted was the truth. One Thursday night it was very interesting because I called Pietro on my mobile from outside Martin's house. He told me he had been on the Skype meeting with Pastor D and the gang and that he had been at Martin's house during the meeting. Well he obviously wasn't at Martin's because we were there, and his van wasn't! I didn't say anything, but he was caught in the first lie I could prove. So, where was he? He could be anywhere.

As he clearly wasn't at Martin's this made the next part easy. Ali and I would check out Matilde's address. I had an idea of where she lived because I had looked on Pietro's Satnav for an address in the East End when I first got suspicious of them the previous summer. I knew she lived in Bow.

I had noticed that a Bow address kept coming up on the Satnav, so one day I confronted him about it. He told me that he had taken the chairs there to Matilde's' home so that she could restore them. I had been upset and made a fuss back then and that he wasn't to go back there again to pick them up. He said he wouldn't and that he would send a courier company to collect them. I managed to look on the Satnav again a couple of weeks or so later and that address had come up again! I had confronted him about this, and he got angry that I didn't trust him, and he denied it. I hated feeling this way. It was making me nuts and acting in ways I would rather not.

Ali and myself headed for the road in Bow that I had noted down and we thought we would find the address easily. Instead that road was long and the number of the road didn't exist as we found out later. We couldn't see Pietro's van anywhere. We realised it was like looking for a needle in a haystack, so we went home. The next day I asked the private investigator friend to look up anything under her name, but they drew a blank. No one of that name existed. We drove around there for a couple of nights with no joy. Suddenly, a day or so later I got a call and am told that Pietro had just got a new address and it was about 800 meters from my flat in Chelsea. I was gobsmacked!

He had moved around the corner and he hadn't told me. The PI said he had only moved within the last couple of days. Then I remembered Pietro had asked me a couple of weeks prior if he was still on my council tax. Now I realised why. Well at least it would be easier to see if he was bringing Matilde to the new flat, now he was conveniently close. Ali said my car was too recognisable if we were going to sit in that street looking out for him. We decided to hire a car and Ali suggested we follow him straight from work one night. That's exactly what we did. We hired a car and when we went to pick it up, we were upgraded to a bigger car which by chance had tinted back windows! We couldn't believe our luck. Ali would drive it and I would sit in the back. We parked by Pietro's van, close to the time the showroom was closing. It was nerve wracking!

He came out. We both ducked. I don't know why Ali did because he would never expect her to be there, she was working in the Ukraine as far as he knew. We followed him and he went to one of the auction houses in Wandsworth/ Battersea area. He unloaded some items and then he loaded a large canvas. I recognised it as one of Matilde's paintings. The auction house hadn't sold it. I'm not surprised, the energy that comes off it was like Helga's. He got in the van and drove off. Then the crunch would come once we went over the bridge and got near to the Embankment. If he went left, he would be going to his new flat and if he went right, he would be heading to Matilde's in Bow. He went right...

Ali kept on his tail and incredibly we didn't lose him. He pulled into a petrol station halfway to Bow and we followed him in and parked. When he came out a few minutes later he had three or four bags of food shopping. That hurt.

It was a Friday night, Friday the 13th of February. I rang Pastor B on the way, and she said I shouldn't be following him and that I should leave it to God. I was not very polite, and I said I had left it to God for too long and I was going to find out for myself. I respect Pastor B, and all that she had done for me in the way of prayers and emotional support. However, when a woman is hurting, and a marriage is at stake, and you love your husband, not everything you do will be rational. I needed the truth, no matter how much it hurt, so I could have closure and move on.

I also called my mother and she told us to be careful. I said I would keep her posted. We followed Pietro all the way to Bow and he pulled off the long road we had been driving up and down on previous nights. No wonder we couldn't find it, his destination was off another road. He then parks by these three big council blocks and walks in. We parked further down the road and waited for five minutes. We then get out and head into the council blocks.

I had number 4 written down from the information collected from his Satnav. They were massive blocks and we decided to investigate all the number 4's of each of the three blocks. One had an Indian family living there, another was a black family, and no one was in at the other one. Ali said we should stay and see if he leaves or stays the night just for irrefutable proof. I said no, I was not going to waste my time over that man anymore.

I had all the proof I needed. She said he would just deny it or have an excuse. So, I said I would call his mobile and see if he answers. It was a long shot and I didn't think he would answer but he did. He sounded cheerful and asked me how I was. I said I wasn't feeling too great. He inquired why.

I said, "Because I am standing outside by your van while you are in Matilde's flat."

Dead silence. I would have loved to have been a fly on the wall of her flat. After about a minute I said, "You need to come out now or I am going to start yelling and asking the neighbours which flat she lives in."

He comes out and he is smoking a cigarette. He looks very nervous and so he should be. He starts telling us, "It's not what it looks like!"

I was quite calm at this stage and said, "What does it look like Pietro? It's a Friday night, you drive to Bow, you stop to buy food shopping and you come to your employee's flat."

He said she was restoring some items and he had bought a couple of pizzas. I said you had four bags of food shopping. I told him he was pure evil because he had been telling everyone that I was such a bad wife, that I was abusive and I had not been looking after him. While all along he was the one sleeping with his employee as I had alleged from the beginning. I told him to bring Matilde downstairs because I wanted to talk to her. I was incandescent with rage. He was trying to calm me down. It was impossible by now after nearly driving me to a breakdown and all the turning myself inside out to try to save our so-called Christian marriage. Me trying to fix everything that he complained about and him telling me that he wasn't interested in this 'silly girl.' Putting me through counselling he had no intention of seeing through, telling me God was with us and he was reading the bible.

I told him to get her to come down and talk to me. Ali was standing as a barrier between us as she didn't want Pietro to lay a finger on me. It was the other way around I was trying to get hold of him to slap him. He was telling Ali that he wasn't having an affair. That set me off. He was caught with his pants down. Lies, lies and more lies.

I started to shout "Matilde come out now. Running around with a married man you should be ashamed of yourself! You are a disgusting, horrible woman! Get down here now," I was vibrating with anger.

The neighbours started coming out. Pietro was embarrassed. Good. Someone opened the main door to the block of flats and I ran as fast as I could towards it to get inside. I would knock on every door until I found her if I had to. Pietro caught up with me and held me back. We were tussling. I said it didn't matter because I would come back the next day and the next and wait to talk to her. In the past Pietro used to get jealous if men tried to talk to me or showed any interest in dating me yet here he was sleeping with this woman and he didn't expect me to do anything?

He said he would call my mother. I said please do. She will have a lot to say to you. There was an impasse for ages. Suddenly Pietro took off out of the council estate and it was the cue for us to go as I have had enough. As we came out of the estate, we saw Pietro in his van talking animatedly to someone. I guessed it was his parents.

We watched him for a couple of minutes. He got out of the van, I told Ali to get the car and I walked towards him and I heard out of nowhere a voice in my heart clearly say, 'Ask him if she is pregnant.' Everything was in free fall. This can't be happening. I asked him. He looked startled but denied it of course. I walked away and got into the car with Ali and we drove off at speed.

Ten minutes later my mum called informing me that Pietro had called her to complain about what had just happened, as if she was going to be sympathetic. She lost it and called him a liar and slammed the phone down on him. He had told her his parents told him to call the police. Mum said call the police she couldn't care. She knows I can handle myself. A police report would have been good for me in an upcoming divorce case.

I then called Pastor D who was in the US and told him what had just happened. He was truly shocked. He more than anyone wanted to believe Pietro was not having an affair. He had warned him against it, he received and suspected it but still didn't want to believe it. He can see things very clearly but somehow the enemy had put a veil of doubt in place. He wasn't sure that me following him there was a good idea or enough proof as I hadn't found him on top of her and she wasn't pregnant! Half an hour later Pastor D called to say Pietro had also called and told him the situation wasn't what it looked like. You couldn't make this up.

Pietro must have called me 50 times on my way home, I did not answer. He kept leaving voice messages and they got more and more angry. He was screaming, "It's divorce, it's divorce!"

His behaviour was absolutely unbelievable. It was as though he had caught me with another man that he had suspected I was having an affair with for months. Ali couldn't get her head round it either. It had been a harrowing evening.

We didn't sleep much that night. I felt vindicated at last. However, I couldn't understand why Pietro had to concoct this elaborate charade. He could have just told me that he had developed feelings for someone else and wanted a divorce. The Christian church does not agree to divorce, so he had to make me the villain of the piece by trying to make out that I was mistreating him in order to get the divorce. I knew all along what was happening.

He was trying to orchestrate it so it looked like he had left me because I was acting unreasonably and then pretend, after a few months, that he and Matilde had started a relationship after we had split up. So, he would be the poor abused husband and she wouldn't be seen as a marriage wrecker. That is exactly what they tried to do. Most people saw through it and knew he was having an affair.

I don't know how much his family and friends in Italy knew because they couldn't see how it was all unfolding over here. I think his parents knew he was seeing her and that he was visiting her the night I caught them out. Again, decent people acting out of character? I had an idea what was driving them.

The next few days were fuzzy. Thank goodness for Ali. She kept me from totally going under. I think she found it hard to see the state I was in. To try and make light of this situation Ali said we should set ourselves up as private investigators. We couldn't believe how we had managed to follow Pietro so successfully.

Ali was amazing. She advised me to write a letter to Pietro's parents saying that they had ignored me when I had asked for help. I told them that this woman was the cause of our marriage breakdown and that I didn't know where my husband was living and obviously it was with this woman, and that they must have had an idea about this. We had had a happy marriage until she came along. His father wrote an unpleasant email back criticising me which infuriated my mother and she wrote back telling Pietro's father off. It was all very sad.

I blocked Pietro on Facebook because I didn't want him to know what I was doing. He would call me in an attempt to make out nothing was going on with Matilde. One night he texted me at 3:45 a.m. saying he had a dream I was having a relationship with my Australian ex, Greg and he was upset! I occasionally spoke to Greg in Australia but it was just to catch-up and general chat. With all that was going on when did I have a chance to go to Australia in that time frame? Anyway, it was none of his business. I had no idea what was going through Pietro's mind.

I was waiting for Matilde to message me and say something about that night. Obviously if nothing was going on between her and Pietro she should have reached out to me with an explanation and to offer me security that she was not involved with my husband. Her silence spoke volumes. I had lost her number from the very early days when she first came to work for us. I had upgraded my phone and lost a whole load of numbers including hers so I had never been able to speak to her directly and he wouldn't give me her number again. I found her on Facebook and sent her a message which stated that I had expected her to contact me since the night I came to her flat and found Pietro there. Any decent person would have called or messaged me to say that I didn't have to worry. I told her she knew exactly what she was doing with her ugly and disturbing painting. I told her God's justice would prevail.

This was a warning in effect. I had every conviction that it would prevail as He had never failed me in the past. In fact, it was quite incredible how hard 'justice' would come down on people in the past who had hurt me. I never had to do anything. I never wished it on anyone.

As a Child-of-God, I am protected, and vengeance is His. Sometimes I would have to pray for God to have mercy on them! Something awful would always happen to them without fail. My pastor told me that people who had hurt or insulted me would be dealt with and I didn't have to give them any thought. That was why I was so scared for Pietro. If he was as innocent as I thought he was, and we were the victims of black magic, his life would be spared. If he was just a cheating husband, it would not. As for people less evolved like poor Ken who messed with dark forces and came up against us - good luck.

Matilde didn't contact me about my message to her, but my husband did! He asked why I was sending Matilde messages like that and tried to explain that she was just a friend. I asked him why he was calling me and not her? I then texted Martin and a couple of people who I thought were covering for them and told them what I thought of them. After all their denial and complicity; to only find out I was right along.

Martin called me and asked why didn't I accept that the marriage was over?

I said, "Why was Pietro still calling and texting me? How dare you talk to me like that, what if I interfered in your marriage?" I slammed the phone down.

I was only looking for truth and concrete proof so I could get my release.

Two months later, sometime in April, on my way to work I got off the tube and got a call from my mum saying Pietro was trying to call me and it was urgent. Obviously, he couldn't get me on the tube. As soon as I finished talking to her a call came in from him. What he told me nearly stopped my heart.

He told me that one of my oldest and closest friends, Don had died in suspicious circumstances. I walked up the stairs to the office and they took one look at me and knew something was wrong. In tears I said I had to go home, turned on my heels and went back down the stairs again. Something had been bugging me in the last few days as I had tried to call Don because he had given me storage space in his garage and I wanted to retrieve some of my items. He normally got back to me very quickly. We had last seen each other at my birthday dinner, about ten days before. He had been in great spirits. One of the runners that supplies the emporium was also Don's neighbour and that was how Pietro had found out what had happened. Don had been found in his flat when his front door was left open. When he was discovered he looked as if was asleep on the sofa.

The police had to make enquiries. He was only in his 50s. I was devastated. We met in a doctor's surgery many years ago when we were both pharmaceutical reps in the Midlands. Both of our fathers were GPs. He had come to stay with Cashmore and myself when we had lived in Hong Kong and we had stayed with his mother for a few days when we went on holiday to Sri Lanka. We had another connection as we both worked for Pfizer. I was going into the company as he was about to leave.

The other coincidence was that my friend, Lily, ended up working for the same pharmaceutical company as Don before he passed. They had become friends too. Lily was distraught. We both attended his funeral along with Elsa another friend who had worked with him in the industry. He was a beautiful soul.

Pietro had suggested we meet to talk about Don a couple of days after he gave me the news, which we did, and things were calm between us. We talked about Don and the last time I saw him. Then suddenly Pietro was talking about love and that I should have told him more often. He was still telling people like a broken record I only loved him 50% and he loved me 100%. A couple of days after we met to discuss Don's passing Pietro calls and tells me he has signed divorce papers. Such great timing. Did he have a heart left?

I had put Karen on standby to help me with the papers when they came. My pastors told me I could not be party to the divorce and I should not agree to it. I was torn and just decided to ride things as they came.

Ali got a job back in Ukraine and with great sadness I said goodbye to her. It was best to keep busy and that was what I tried to do. The wheels and cogs in my brain were slowing down and I felt I needed to see my counsellor, Alex, who had helped me in the past. I attended my Skype meetings with Pastor D and RM as they had moved to Atlanta in the US. Thank goodness Pastor B was still here. However, she was taking regular trips back to Nigeria, but I could talk to her regularly on my spare phone with a sim card for foreign calls.

Eventually the divorce petition for my unreasonable behaviour arrived, there had been a problem with the delivery. I opened it and I could not believe its contents.

It was a total piece of fiction. It was like the previous letter Pietro had sent me, but worse. It said I was a jealous and abusive drunk, who was terrible with money, never helped him in the business and I kept accusing him of having an affair. It said my parents hadn't been good to him. The bit about my parents broke my heart as they had treated him like a son. Pietro received an irate phone call from me. I told him he should be ashamed of himself, he didn't know what to say for himself. I just hung up.

125

The petition was dated 10th April 2015.

My solicitor took instructions and my behaviour as being unreasonable was refuted. My pastors were still maintaining that I should not agree to the divorce. Pastor D called Pietro's father and asked him as a lay pastor how he could entertain divorce? He said that as a Christian everyone should be trying to keep the marriage together and that since Pietro was saying there was no relationship with Matilde then we should be able to work it out. His father was not helpful. We all knew the truth. It was stalemate. There was no way I was going to agree to a divorce based on my unreasonable behaviour. I was biding my time and there was a reason for this.

## PINK TRICYCLE

Things usually happened on the 13 day of the month.

Some of Pietro's mail was still coming to my flat so occasionally I would get my home help to drop it off or on the rare occasion if it looked urgent, I would post it through the letter box of his basement flat around the corner. On June 13th, 2015 a letter arrived for Pietro so I went to drop it through the letterbox of the flat. I walked down the metal staircase and as I turned around to go back up, I saw a child's pink tricycle under the stairs. It was for a child the same age group as Matilde's daughter by Salva.

I saw red. I went down the road to the Emporium and into Pietro's showroom, I almost ran. He was sitting in the mezzanine. He got a shock when he saw me.

I asked in the calmest voice I could muster who the pink tricycle belonged to. He was fast on his feet. He said it belonged to a neighbour's child. I asked him why the neighbours would put it there? He was squirming. I called him a liar and I asked him if he was even reading his bible these days or did he have some excuse for that too.

126

I looked him straight in the eye and asked if he was having a relationship with Matilde because if he was, he could have his divorce. All I wanted was the truth. I wanted him to just do the decent thing and tell me. He couldn't look at me but continued to deny it. I said that adultery was the only ground where a Christian could be justified in divorce, but he was not getting one on trumped up allegations for my unreasonable behaviour. It was a matter of principle as far as I was concerned. I walked out.

Two things were holding me back. If I thought Pietro was a simple liar and cheat, I would have walked away long before now. It was obvious he was completely under the forces of darkness. I was not going to be his scapegoat. It was maddening, he continued to tell family and friends the nonsense that was outlined in the divorce petition.

As if that wasn't enough at the same time, I was made redundant by the company I was working for. It had got bad press and suddenly ceased operating. This was another shock as I needed the income to pay my mortgage and bills as I was getting nothing from Pietro. It was easier not going for maintenance because I had more to lose if he came after my flat in the divorce. Though he had said he would never try to take my flat I couldn't trust him because of his latest actions. There was no way I was in a fit state to look for a new job, I was just about managing to do the last one on autopilot. In fact, I had gone back to counselling with the same counsellor and she could see I was struggling.

I was signed off sick for several months. I was then told I had to go to an interview for an assessment of my health. They decided that my ESA had to stop even though I still had a sickness certificate covering me for a few more weeks. They told me I had to go onto Jobseekers allowance when it was quite clear I couldn't function. I honestly don't know how people cope or manage in this current climate in similar situations. The whole system is broken and needs to be changed as many vulnerable people are being placed in very stressful positions with no money or back up. Recently there have been very tragic cases of people committing suicide because of this.

Thank goodness for my parents, I don't know where I would be without them. I wish that everyone who needs support could get it. My parents decided I didn't need to go back to work as I was in no fit state and that they would support me until I got back on my feet and was stronger emotionally. Also, they needed my help to relocate to London. I was spending a great deal of time going backwards and forwards to Birmingham because my parents had decided to sell their house and move into their London flat. Dad was getting frailer and mum wanted to be nearer to her children and grandchildren. She wanted support and she also wanted to make sure I was okay. They had lived in their house for over fifty years and there was so much stuff in that house.

It took months to sift through everything, to decide what we wanted to keep, throw away or give to charity. The house was taken off the market for a while as we sorted the house and its contents. It was decided that after our yearly family holiday to Portugal my parents would move to London in September. In the meantime, we would go to Birmingham to continue to empty the house for a week at a time. We would put it on the market in the New Year. This kept me busy and my mind off my problems.

## CAUGHT

August 13th, 2015.

I had an appointment in Fulham and I usually park my car on the road where Pietro's flat is or the next road up. His flat is on the border before it goes into the Borough of Hammersmith and Fulham and my car permit is for Kensington and Chelsea. This was my usual parking spot for years long before he moved there and I was not going to go the long way around just to avoid his flat.

It was a nice, sunny day and I walked past the flat. I noticed that the blind was up and the window half open. The child's pink tricycle was attached to the railings. That got my hackles up. Running late for my appointment took my focus. However, on the way back from my appointment God put in my heart me to knock on the door and I would discover more. I wasn't sure what to do so I got to the car and sat inside for several minutes pondering on what to do. If in doubt I always call my pastors. I called Pastor B who advised me as she did before, not to do anything in haste.

I drove to my flat, parked outside and sat in the car for another few minutes thinking. It's not often that I get such clear instructions. I drove back to his flat, parked the car and walked down the metal stairs to the basement and rang the bell. This was now early afternoon so Pietro should have been at work and would not have left the window open.

I heard a woman's voice indicating that she was coming to answer the door. I recognised the voice. It was Matilde. She opens the door and had to do a double take, she was so shocked.

She gasped, "Oh, Gita."

"Oh yes it's Gita," I said.

It all happened in a couple of seconds, I glanced down and there she was, about six months pregnant. Nothing had prepared me for that. It was horrendous. No more speculation or lies. The awful truth was right there in front me.

I felt nauseous and I was shaking. She tried to slam the door on me, but adrenaline was flowing through my veins. She is a big girl, stocky, but my strength came from above, and once again fuelled by the rage I find myself in during these situations which had been consistently blindsiding me. I pushed the door so hard she flew backwards. I verbally laid into her. I wanted to go for her but held myself back because she was pregnant, and I was now in Pietro's flat.

I ordered her to call Pietro on the phone and to get him to come to the flat now! Then to my amazement there was the biggest black cat sitting in the corner. Firstly, most Italians don't like black cats, they find them to be bringers of bad luck, so I was told. Secondly, Pietro doesn't like cats, he threw out one of his ex-girlfriend's cats from her flat because he is highly allergic to them. I called her a witch and that she was casting spells and that she was demonic as well as her ugly paintings. I told her it was no surprise her ex-boyfriend had dumped her and the baby. I asked her how long did she think it would last with Pietro once he woke up?

I told her God reveals things to me and asked her if she thought I would never find out? This was just the start and He would deal with her sooner or later. I said God did not build this house and it would not stand. It got really heated and her daughter was in the other room, which I didn't realize, she ran to the door where we stood and started crying.

I toned it down and Matilde told her to go back to the bedroom. Then the fracas continued and in the middle of it all someone comes to the door and this Jezebel goes to answer it! I was speechless. Obviously, it wasn't Pietro because he would have a key. I can hear her talking to a woman. After months of carrying on with my husband, she hasn't apologised, or tried to explain. Matilde has no shame.

She is talking to what looks like a neighbour. I go up behind Matilde and say over her shoulder to this woman, "Hello I am Pietro's wife and this slut is his employee, who he has denied having an affair with for months. Quite clearly you can see she is pregnant. Please tell the whole street."

This poor woman doesn't know what to do. I walk back to the lounge. At this point Pietro arrives. He was sweating and was close to tears. He says to me the relationship has only just started.

"Look at her… she is six months pregnant!!" I retorted.

The air went blue. He said he was going to tell me about the 'brand new' relationship. He really believed his own lies. Then he told her off in Italian that she shouldn't have left the pink bicycle outside because I had seen it and the game was up. He forgot I understood quite a bit of Italian.

The dynamic between them was very odd. He was talking to her like she was a school child and there was no warmth or connection. It got incredibly volatile and Matilde threatened to call the police. I told her to carry on because I wasn't going anywhere until I finished what I had to say.

She grabs the phone and is dialling away. Pietro pulls it out of her hand and throws it across the floor. Within two minutes there's another knock on the door and it is the police. They want to know what is going on. I explain that I am Pietro's wife and that I have just found out that he has been having an affair with his employee and that he has denied it for months. I explain that Pietro can't deny it because she is pregnant, and I only live around the corner and must deal with this. The female officer goes into the bedroom with Pietro and Matilde, and the male officer stays with me in the lounge. He is nice and asks if I was alright.

I tell him that naturally I was very upset and shocked about what I discovered. He asked me if I wanted anything. He said he couldn't believe that a man would move his mistress in just around the corner from his wife. That he comes across men who behave this badly every now and again. He wanted to know how many months pregnant she was. He thought four and I said six. The realization also hit me that the voice I heard on the night of Friday February 13th was a warning of what was to come. God was preparing me. That was six months earlier and maybe Pietro knew she was pregnant then or he may not. I was even more furious because looking at the size of her bump she would have been a couple of months pregnant when Pietro had filed his divorce petition on me for my unreasonable behaviour. In it he stated that I was jealous and was accusing him of having an affair!

131

Pulling me out of that train of thought I hear Pietro say something about prosecco from the other room. The policeman couldn't stop me. I ran into the corridor asked him what was he trying to imply? He was trying to make out I had gone around there because I must have been drinking prosecco and was drunk in the middle of the afternoon! I was incensed.

"Stop lying about me drinking. You are the one who is the drinker," I said. This is probably what he had told Matilde, that I was a drunk. I told them all that Pietro was constantly texting me and in one of the texts he mentioned that he wasn't happy. You should have seen the look on Matilde's face. She gave him such a filthy look. The policeman asked me to show him. I had so many texts from Pietro I had to keep paging down. Matilde was not impressed. He probably told her he had no contact with me and yet there were tons of texts. I found the text and the policeman read out the one that said Pietro wasn't happy.

It was time to go and I made some passing comment to Matilde about how this wasn't finished as I left. I felt even more betrayed than I believed possible as I left with the two police officers. It was humiliating, as if I was being escorted out by the police. At least I finally knew the truth. Pietro could not lie his way out of this. He was well and truly caught.

# CHAPTER 10

—⊶◇⊷—

# AFTERMATH

I think that me finally catching the two of them was a huge jolt for Pietro. He was beside himself. He was calling and texting me asking why I didn't tell him that I loved him. He said he couldn't stop crying. I told him he was only crying because he got caught.

I couldn't help it, but I messaged Matilde a few things that I thought she should know. She probably fell for Pietro telling her we were not having relations! It gave me some satisfaction that he didn't seem to be happy with Matilde, but he had made his bed and he had to lie in it. That was a term used by some people. Everyone could see it. Many people had said that he had completely changed, he wasn't the same happy go lucky person and that he was always miserable and angry at work. It was even commented upon that it was like the devil was inside him. Little did they know.

They said it would never last between him and Matilde. That was a given.

Pietro had told his friends that there was nothing going on between him and Matilde, and so when they discovered that he lied they were shocked with the level of deceit. They were not the only ones. Pastor D and Pastor B even though they already had a knowing that this was happening were stunned that she was about six months pregnant. And also, that he had lied to them until the end. They were very hurt by this.

I wrote to him and his parents' explaining that now that I was in possession of the facts, I didn't spare them. I said they had sold their souls for a grandchild and how angry and appalled I was at their son's schemes. I said that they should watch out and see what God was going to do because Pietro had behaved like David with Bathsheba sending Uriah to the front line to be killed so that they could have their affair.

I told them Matilde was lucky I hadn't laid into her and as I had told them all along that she was a witch and doing witchcraft and black magic on their son. It was cathartic to get it off my chest. This was a battle and I was not going to keep quiet or play nice.

My mother also wrote to Pietro and his parents expressing her feelings on this whole sorry matter.

After the drama of it all, I fell into a trance like state. The trauma took its toll. My parents had been shocked by the pregnancy but not surprised at the affair, they were concerned for my health and mental state, as were my friends. I think at the time my friends would have lynched Pietro if they could for stringing me along and trying to put the reason for our divorce onto me. One of my friends asked me how can anyone ever get over something like that?

I was so thankful that it was that time of year and we were flying out to Portugal for the family holiday within the next few days. That was the only thing that kept me going, the fact I would be away from all of this for three weeks. I don't remember anything about that holiday except that I cried in my room a lot and moved around like a zombie.

Coming back to England was not easy.

# ROAD TO RECOVERY

The long road to recovery commenced. My parents wanted to wrap me up in cotton wool. They tried to keep me occupied and were worried because, as most people in times of stress, I lost my appetite and mum kept trying to make me eat. It was difficult to sleep. They decided we should all join The Chelsea Harbour Club, which is the local gym in my area because my brother had been a member since the early 1990s. I didn't argue because I didn't want to go to my gym anymore, Virgin Active in Chelsea, Pietro was still going there. I had been a member since 1995 when it was the original Holmes Place, so I was sad to leave.

Chelsea Harbour Club has the best spa and I would spend long periods of time in there trying to forget my woes. It kept me from losing my mind! As did my pastors who were there for me. I would go to see Pastor B or talk to Pastor D on Skype. A little time was spent with friends as I wasn't feeling sociable. Sleeping, reading and watching sci-fi became the norm, as well as watching Joyce Meyer and Joel Osteen on TV. Also, my parents needed help with their new life in London. They really missed their Birmingham friends and still do.

Another situation which needed sorting out was the actual divorce. My solicitor, Karen, was trying to steer me in the right direction over the divorce. Previously when I couldn't prove adultery, I was adamant that Pietro would not get a divorce for my unreasonable behaviour. Now the truth had surfaced at last I told him to drop the fake allegations he had made, and he could have his divorce for his adultery. This would have been fought out in court, but my solicitor said that would be a costly, protracted matter.

I wasn't happy at all because in effect I had to agree to these fake allegations because of cost. There was no justice in this. We both had to agree to each other's petitions in the end. These no fault divorces and quickie divorces are not helping society!

Pietro and Matilde's plan had been that Pietro would get his divorce quickly after pretending to everyone that they had got together after we split up. Because she was pregnant, they had been planning to get married asap and fudge her dates for pregnancy because it's against Christian principles to have a child out of wedlock or to have been living in sin if you strictly follow the bible.

The plan was thwarted because there was not going to be a quick divorce until God helped me unravel the plan and expose it. They couldn't get married; her pregnancy was too far gone and there was no divorce in sight. I was in awe because my pastors always said I would be vindicated, and I was. Part of me felt a bit better and the other part felt incredibly sad at whatever the spirit was that was possessing Pietro was driving him to plot, plan and behave like this. After they were exposed whenever I had to drive past their road, I heard the words 'No joy,' or 'Desolation,' loud and clear. For me this was a time of more divine revelation.

## GOOD FRIENDS

My friends were brilliant. They rallied around me and constantly called me or tried to get me out and about. I must admit I wasn't ready to socialise and was turning into a bit of a hermit. I think when dark periods in life come upon us quiet reflection and reassessment of life is natural.

Once again Ali came to England to stay with me to pick up some things she had previously left with me but mostly to see how I was doing. My latest discovery had left her stunned and angry. She was only in the UK for a few days but said she was going to make the time to visit Pietro at the Emporium. I couldn't stop her.

I had gone to a friend's birthday lunch when Ali decided to pay Pietro a visit. Ali hadn't come back by the time I had returned from my lunch appointment so I wondered what was taking her so long. Twenty minutes later Ali returned as white as a ghost and clearly very upset. She had to sit down for a few minutes. She told me in short that she spoke to Pietro nicely but firmly and told him that she was very saddened that he had every opportunity to tell me the truth and he hadn't taken it, and that he had lied to her as well.

She was gentle with him and apparently, he had put his head on his desk and just cried for ages. He was sorry for what he had done. This had really shaken Ali. She liked Pietro a great deal and thought he was a good guy. It was all so out of character for him. When she told me this I was upset too because, as usual, I hated to think of Pietro in pain.

This took a bit of a twist when the legal proceedings kicked off, he had construed Ali's visit to him as me having sent her there and that I was ready to divorce on the grounds of my unreasonable behaviour. She had to put in writing to my solicitor that was not the case and that she went to see him to get an understanding of why he had allowed everything to happen as it did. His mood swings being evidence of the duality of the personality inhabiting him.

My friend, Dina, was also upset with Pietro because he had repeatedly lied to her about not having an affair with Matilde. She had seen them together in the little park next to the Emporium a few months before and had gone up to speak to them. She said she had interrupted something because he had looked very annoyed and Matilde had looked down or depressed. She had also told me months before that Pietro had approached her when he had been looking for a flat.

Dina is in the property business and has several properties which she lets out. She told Pietro that I was her friend and she would not help him get a flat away from his wife. I was grateful for her loyalty. She would bump into Pietro now and then as her flat was on the road that borders one side of his place of work. She would chat to him and a couple of times he had told her he still loved me and always thought of me.

After the truth came out, she asked Pietro if he even loved Matilde and he didn't answer. She repeated her question and this time he said he was "Working on it!" Dina told him that she could see absolutely no connection between him and Matilde. I was fuming when she told me this. I called him and said, "You have done all of this for a woman you can't even say that you love and are treating as a baby making machine?"

Dina was always there at pivotal times. She also bumped into them just two weeks after the baby was born, which was a real eye opener, as that was in mid-November 2015 which going exactly nine months back, meant the baby was conceived in mid-February 2015! Pietro had not wanted this to come out and even with the maths he kept denying it. I had been spot on when I had asked him if Matilde was pregnant the night Ali and myself had followed him.

Dina is glamorous and Matilde had asked her how she knew Pietro. She told her she was a close friend of mine. A conversation took place where Dina told Pietro that he should do the decent thing and not go after my flat in the divorce proceedings and any settlement. It was clear to everyone what had been going on and that I didn't deserve what they had done. Matilde rolled her eyes and walked off. Dina again said there was no connection between them. Dina always says what she thinks. She is a good friend to have.

Another loyal friend, Anton, staged an intervention. I had known him since the early Nineties. Before I tell you how he helped me I'll give you a bit of background on my creative pursuits which is how I actually met Anton.

My sister and myself had gone to a gig and met Anton there. This is going back more years than I care to remember. He was unusual back then because he was a white guy with the longest blond dreadlocks we had ever seen. As he was a musician and a DJ, we ended up knowing some of the same people on the scene. Those were the days when I had started to make headway in acting and the music industry.

The creative arts have always been my passion. I attended an intensive summer course in acting at Webber Douglas Drama School in Kensington, just down the road from me and I was encouraged to do the Post Graduate course by one of the tutors there. I really wanted to do this but then I reached a crossroads as my then partner, Cashmore had secured a post at Hong Kong University. I was torn between my relationship and my career. This would be a recurring theme in my life. I decided to go to Hong Kong as it was also an opportunity to travel extensively. Besides there may be some opportunities over there singing or acting and I was only going for a year I thought and then come back to the UK to continue with my training.

Hong Kong was a mixed experience, a fascinating place, I couldn't get my head around how so many people were crammed into such a small space. To keep us sane, Cashmore made sure we went away every few weeks to Macau for weekends, mainland China or further afield to Thailand, Sri Lanka or the Philippines. Looking back those were magical times and I am grateful to him for showing me many beautiful parts of the world. Within a short space of time I got involved on the drama scene and took part in plays and joined the Garrison Players. Through Cashmore's contacts I managed to get some press coverage which was fun.

We were there for nearly two years and for various reasons that was long enough. In the end a position opened for Cashmore as a Professor at the University of Tampa, Florida in the US. He took it and it was agreed he would go but I would stay in the UK. Cashmore relocated to the States and it was incredibly difficult, but I had to get my head down and concentrate on what to do next to make my dream happen. Within a month of returning to the UK I went on holiday to Puerto Pollensa, Mallorca with my Aunty M and her two lovely daughters.

This was the playground for the rich and famous in those days. I met some interesting people whilst I was on holiday one of them being an investment banker from London, Arthur, whose brother was Tony Ponte who had previously been high up in Decca Records in the US and he was now involved in films.

One night we were in a bar called Brisas and I remember singing along to one of the songs and Tony came over to me and started talking. What he said captured my interest. He liked my voice and wanted to talk to me about it. It was arranged that we would meet up in London to discuss this further.

I met Tony as planned in London and we signed a five-year music management contract. It started making me think about my direction, I really cared for Tony and he wanted a relationship however I was still with Cashmore so that was not a possibility. He then wanted me to go to Australia with him as he was working on a film project and I declined as I had just moved back from Hong Kong and didn't want to travel to the other side of the world again. The contract was binding but didn't say I had to relocate. It was decided that Barry who was a close friend of Tony's' would look after me in his absence. Barry was a hugely influential businessman and we became great friends. Time was ticking and Tony was in Australia longer than any of us expected and I couldn't sit around waiting. Barry put it to Tony that it wasn't fair on me and negotiated a way out of the contract for me. It was all very amicable. Barry and another business associate of his, Phil, were prepared to put up £500,000 to launch my career and put out a single.

To advance and improve my singing career I was an introduced to Helena Shenel. She is no doubt the best vocal coach around and became a very dear and close friend. She was teaching George Michael at the time, as well as Paul Young, Lulu, Peter Gabriel and countless others. Helena has had a big influence on my life.

I had some wonderful opportunities to perform on national television in Europe which my parents were very proud of since they had no idea my career was taking off. As my career began to advance, I met and worked with amazing respected producers such as, Talvin Singh, Charles Bailey and Danny Chang, who were all instrumental in my development. Nitin

Sawhney was a good friend and a big influence.

I turned my attention to the US and secured British management based in LA. I had become disillusioned with the UK and hoped to get signed in the US and was so close. I wrote songs with the producer of the Bay Watch albums who had the same management as myself, and who wrote hits for Blue and Sugar Babes.

Something always prevented my big break. I couldn't understand why things weren't going my way. It got too much. I decided to put music on the back burner for a while and concentrate on keeping my head down and to continue working as a pharmaceutical rep. There were other creative forays with great promise but then they would fizzle out. How could one person be so unlucky?

# CHAPTER 11

———————)( )(———————

## HOLDING ONTO SANITY

Going back to Anton, like myself he would never give up music but had to turn his attention to paying bills and getting a proper job. He joined Landmark Education. He tried to get me to enrol more than 20 years ago and I backed out after paying a deposit. So, years on and my marriage had fallen apart and I was a mess, he couldn't stand on the side-lines any longer. He persuaded me to meet a friend of his called Stella, who would talk to me about what Landmark was all about. I was sceptical at first but after I listened to what she had to say, I asked him why he hadn't dragged me to a presentation year earlier. I learned a very simple solution to most people's problems. It was separating 'The story' from 'The facts.' This really helped my mental state and Anton was also proving himself to be a caring and loyal friend.

Now that Anton had finally got me to understand that there had been a quicker and easier way to process the trials and tribulations of life that no one escapes and after attending Stella's taster session on what Landmark had to offer, there was no stopping me.

I enrolled on the first of three programmes, The Forum, the Advanced course and then finally the Self Expression and Leadership Course. The last course really got me focused on one area of social injustice in particular, food waste was my chosen project. I have long had a bee in my bonnet, I believe that not one person needs to starve in our world.

I learnt a great deal on these courses and met some wonderful people. I was now open to more ways in which I could take the attention off myself and my problems and aspire to become a solution to other people's challenges. This is something I have tried to do in whatever way I could over the years, however small, even if it's to help a friend in need. It doesn't have to be on a large scale. If you are facing challenges and are stuck in a loop obsessing about your problems believe me there are those who have much, much larger ones. It's a great equaliser.

There must be a purpose for our lives and I always thought I knew what mine was and was frustrated that it seemed to be thwarted at every turn. Going through this intense period of strife, I was just about holding onto sanity. It was the reason to re-evaluate what was important to me and that every day should count. A quote resonated with me by an unknown author.

**The Essence of a New Day**

"This is the beginning of a new day.

You have been given this day to use as you will.

You can waste it or use it for good.

What you do today is important.

Because you are exchanging a day of your life for it.

When tomorrow comes, this day will be gone forever.

In its place is something that you have left behind…

Let it be something good."

A friend, Natasha Aylott, invited me to attend a conference where she was speaking. She is a beautiful lady with a heart to see women succeed. At the conference I was drawn to another speaker Tony Dada, whom I made a bee line for, to speak to after his presentation. There was an instant connection. If you want to succeed in life I think it's important, even necessary, to find the right mentor or coach. Tony and myself worked together on a 12-week 1-2-1 programme which helped me enormously. He was instrumental in me really finding out who I was and what I wanted. Simple questions which he didn't let me off until we really drilled down into it. I wanted to be free, free to travel and free financially, like everyone of course!

This took my mind off Pietro. Tony knew what I was going through and could see I was really struggling. He has such a calm and reassuring presence. It was what I needed to be around and just absorb. Tony kindly introduced me to his mentor Brother Ishmael Tetteh who is a man of great wisdom and influence.

I am open to learn from many different areas of life, religions, ideologies and I had learnt long ago to follow my heart and do the things I love to do and not what others want for you or try to impose on you. This was reinforced by working with my mentors. Through Tony I learnt the term, "Creative social entrepreneur." It's a good idea to have mentors for different areas of your life. All this helped me through a particularly tough time, and I recommend working with people who can help you grow and equip you through good times and bad. I am working with three other amazing mentors, Graham W. Price and his Positive Mind Training Program; Simon Rogers, who is helping me to balance my health and improve performance on all levels and Raymond Aaron, who is also a huge influence.

I will keep the passion for learning for as long as I am on this planet.

—

# CHAPTER 12

———×()×———

# LIVING UNDER A CURSE

Up until my thirties I had lived what seemed a charmed life. Then situations started to occur which made me question everything especially regarding my private life. Apart from the impact of other people's untoward behaviour, I often used to think that the powers that be had it in for me.

One day mum admitted that a jealous aunt in India had cursed our family many years ago. I was astonished that she hadn't mentioned this sooner. Mum fluctuates in the belief that negative forces have affected the family and then flipping that and saying that as Children-of-God nothing can harm us. However, it was hard to deny evidence that something supernatural was happening regarding my family. I can't discuss this in detail, but situations have occurred which are not normal especially regarding relationships, finances and health.

No one has escaped.

A while ago my sister was parking her car and a total stranger came up to her and told her there was a curse on her family! He started to tell her things that he couldn't possibly have known about her. She was so freaked out that she called me. I told her about our "aunt story," and I told her to speak to mum about it. I also told her to pray and to check out Derek Prince as I was just discovering him at the time, I told my mum to do the same.

A couple of hours later my mum calls me after watching one of the videos and says, "Yes, we must be under a curse!" I couldn't help being amused because she had changed her stance again and it's what I had been telling her all along. I told her that we just need to know how to overcome curses and negative forces and to keep watching more Derek Prince videos to get relevant information and protect ourselves.

One of his books changed my life, 'Blessings or a Curse You Choose,' a good friend, Karina, who is part of Pastor D's group had recommended this book to me. After I had read it, I was much more enlightened. I was, either through ignorance or unbelief doing everything that the book told people not to do. It explained why certain things could be happening in people's lives. If you remember I had already started removing influences and objects that I had realized were not keeping me on the right path with the help of Pastor D and Pastor B.

The book was clear on removing anything that signified other Gods, idolatry or charms. I had already gotten rid of carvings and statues, which for years I insisted were beautiful objects and insisted that having them around didn't mean that I was worshipping idols. Now with new revelation from Derek Prince, I knew that the Chinese horse and frog ornaments and evil eye trinkets all had to go. I had also stopped going for clairvoyance/fortune telling sessions. Information in the book stopped me dead in the tracks from ever thinking much less ever going to these types of places again.

## GROWING IN KNOWLEDGE

It's a concept which seems simple, honour your mother and father. I think with all the stress I was getting impatient and rude to my parents. This is still something I struggle with. Every day I am praying for the grace and the strength to be patient. Other people were noticing and were not impressed with me. I did notice that I was clashing all the time with my mother which was not normal. It wasn't making sense.

I was telling her she had the same kind of nasty, goading spirit that Pietro had had in him. The realisation that this was another spiritual attack dawned on me, I prayed and asked the pastors to pray for us. Later, I would enlist the help of people at the church. That helped us to stop fighting like cat and dog however, every now and again it comes upon us and I know it is trying to pull us apart and I always get prayer help.

Karina from Pastor D's group had started to go to Holy Trinity Brompton (HTB), a church in Knightsbridge, London. This was the church my mother had been trying to get my siblings and myself to attend for the last 25 years. Karina invited me to join her on the Alpha course, she was one of the group leaders. I decided to go. She was co-leading with Alistair.

I really enjoyed the Alpha course. It gave me comfort and peace in the storm. Karina knew Pietro and was present when our marriage was falling apart. She couldn't believe what was happening but knew it was the supernatural at work. I went away for the Alpha weekend and had a close encounter with the Holy Spirit, though subtle it made me emotional.

On the way back from the Alpha weekend I was in Alistair's car with Greta who attended HTB and was also Karina's friend. The conversation turned to the book Kristina had given me by Derek Prince. I was only halfway through it and had got to the part where he is talking about "Sozo." It is a very deep spiritual cleansing. I had never heard of it before.

I knew I needed it but didn't know what to do or where to go. It was not chance or coincidence, but Greta knew exactly what it was, and she knew a little bit about what had happened with the witchcraft on my marriage. She told me that they do "Sozo" at Holy Trinity Swiss Cottage. I was blown away and ecstatic. After finding the relevant information, an application form had to be submitted. This was done, however, they were very busy, there was at least a three-month waiting list before you could be seen. It was disappointing because help was needed in that instant. So, I just had to wait. It was interesting to know that there were so many other people in need of this sort of help.

Once the Alpha course finished, I joined Alistair's Connect group which he co-led with a lovely lady, Rose. Karina was also in this group and Greta was the administrator for it. I told her I had applied for a Sozo appointment but that I had to wait months for it. In the meantime, it was so good to have this support and I started to make friends in the group, one had been a friend I hadn't seen for many years, Charis. She used to go to my old gym, and another friend was Donna. I had started to come out of my shell and socialise which was great for my mental health.

Eventually the Sozo appointment time came and I went up to Swiss Cottage for it. Pauline and Mira were the ladies who were going to conduct my Sozo. I was told it can take up to three hours.

It was a profound experience. They prayed over me and they asked a series of questions which connected your earthly family to God. They asked about relationships with your parents, to God, Jesus, and the Holy Spirit. Tears were running down my face within a short period of time. God loved me. Before I knew it, three hours later the appointment had come to an end and I hadn't had a chance to pray about what was happening in my marriage and to see if they could shed light on it. They told me to book another appointment so they could pray over my marriage then.

This time I couldn't get a Sozo appointment for nearly six months because they were so booked up. By then a lot had happened. When I went back Pauline and Mira they started to pray and told me I had to renounce everything that was not of God and that I had dabbled into as far back as I could remember and ask for forgiveness.

I got to the part where I was telling them about a woman I had gone to visit for a reading in India who pronounced all these negative things on me and had demanded a lot of money to remove the negativity and I had refused. They had to pray hard about that one. Suddenly it came out that a so-called friend of mine had put a lot of witchcraft on me.

I had started to burp, get stomach cramps and feel sick. Pauline and Mira had to jump out of their seats to come and put their hands on me to pray. It was alarming. Then it hit me. This was what Pietro had been talking about. I sat there quietly taking it in and controlling my emotions. This person was exposed as being part of the motley crew of evil doers who were using their energy to hurt us. My spirit suddenly knew that this person was partly responsible for the death of a close friend of mine and for wrecking my marriage. I would have to apologise to Pietro for not believing him when he said a friend of mine was doing witchcraft on us. I am not even going to put a name to this person, they know who they are.

Pauline and Mira then moved onto me visualising The Court of Heaven. They asked me to imagine I was there and asked what I saw. It looked like a typical criminal court room. I saw Pietro in the dock. I heard the word, 'Innocent,' clearly. I started to cry. Pietro was innocent. They reassured me and encouraged me to continue.

What else did I see or hear? I then heard two words, 'Hope' and 'Revenge.' They said I was safe and to tell them how I felt. I felt immense relief and that I hadn't been wrong. That Pietro had been spellbound and not to be blamed for his actions. It was good to have fresh spiritual eyes on this. They told me to be strong, that revenge was God's and not mine. Whoever was doing this would be taken care of and I had to have hope. I felt freed by the time I left the church.

On the way home, I called Pastor B and told her about the revelation of the fourth woman which had knocked me for six. I had had my suspicions; I knew that this woman was jealous because a friend told me about what she had said about me behind my back, but I never expected that she could be this vindictive. Pastor B told me that this person was evil and that I was never to speak to them again and, as usual, let God deal with them.

I resolved to mention this to Pietro when the time presented itself. I was ill for about three weeks with stomach cramps after my Sozo.

My own spirit had been affected and polluted. I felt I was being cleansed and healed.

I continued with my Tuesday nights at the Connect group at HTB and one Tuesday I was walking towards the meeting when I came alongside this tall, smart black man heading the same way. We said hello and exchanged pleasantries and walked in. The meeting started and turns out he was the guest speaker that night. His name was Louis and he gave an incredible talk on marriage and finding the right wife or husband.

He then started talking about the witchcraft and black magic that had been put on people's marriages to be destroyed. I was amazed as I felt he was directing this at me. Very few people in our group are married or had been married. He then tells everyone who wanted to find a life partner to stand up. Everyone stood up apart from me. I was just going through my divorce! Karina pulls me to my feet though I protested, I told her I was staying clear of men, let alone wanting another husband! We found that amusing.

I had to wait my turn to speak to Louis after his talk as everyone was wanting to talk to him too. He is a powerful, prophetic man. When I got to him, he wanted to pray for me though I had not mentioned anything I was dealing with to him. He said God would cut off the head off the snake and that what God put together let no man or woman put asunder! We had to pray for the 'veil' to be removed from Pietro's eyes. The exact words used by Pastors B, D and various others. All singing from the same hymn sheet. It was confirmation because those words would be used repeatedly.

152

This was the start of a friendship with Louis and me. He set up another Connect group which is on alternate Tuesdays to the current Connect group. His meetings are so anointed, and he is an explosive and inspiring speaker. I was co-leader, however, I travel a lot and can't be there sometimes and Louis has a passion for street evangelism, while mine is for social activism, worship, and writing.

With all of this support my life started to stabilise. My emotions still had more healing to do. Forgiveness was an ongoing process. It was difficult because every now and again I would see Pietro or Matilde. I never saw them together which helped. It was particularly galling when I drove past her pushing a pram. It was hard to avoid as they were living just around the corner. It bothered me, there were plenty of other places they could have gone. It felt deliberate and reinforced Pietro's weird behaviour. Everything felt like it was meant to inflict maximum pain and damage. It was effective.

I tried to keep myself occupied. I had started to renovate my flat just as my divorce had come through. I wanted to rent it out so I could make some income out of it.

Whilst this was going on my parents decided to renovate their flat which was a bigger job than mine. I questioned God a lot in this period. There were several series of unfortunate events that created more headache and financial burdens. Why was all this happening? I knew it was either a major test or, I was still under witchcraft. At this stage I just wanted whatever it was to stop. I had a marriage breakdown, divorce, made redundant, had terrible builders who cost me thousands of pounds, battles with the management committee of my building, nearly lost my flat, court battles, and the deaths of three of my closest friends in a very short space of time.

Add to that the marriage with Greg that was called off, and the death of the man I was with before Pietro. There has been much thought about whether to mention this relationship as he has passed. I have decided it may shed light on whether a curse was operating and whether my inadvertent behaviour added to my situation. The law of cause and effect again.

Liam was a doctor, he gave up general practice to set up a biotech company. We met and at the time he told me he was separated from his wife. He had his own place and he wasn't wearing a wedding ring when I met him. There is no way I would have gone near a married man.

We started to see each other. This was the first time I had been in a relationship with someone who had children. He had three lovely sons who would spend a lot of time with us. His parents treated his ex-wife like she was their daughter and no longer viewed Liam as the golden boy. As time went on, I found out little snippets that maybe he wasn't as straight with me as I thought regarding his ex in the beginning. She made life difficult for us as did his parents. They wouldn't accept me. This tore him apart.

We had an up and down relationship because of this tension. We discovered that he had a huge, very rare tumour in his neck and head. I was with him from diagnosis, trying to find the right specialist to deal with this operation, he made it through but it had serious repercussions. I won't say anymore.

We split up because of the family pressure. We got back together, split up again. It was getting silly. On the final split we didn't see each other or contact each other until just before I was about to marry Pietro in 2009, he wrote me a beautiful card with a golden fairy on it and a message saying that was how he viewed me, spreading magic.

He was trying to get back with me. Pietro tore it up. Liam was then texting me, but I shut it down. Two years after that I am told by friends that he had died. I knew he was ill again but didn't know how badly. If I had known I would have gone to see him to make peace. It was devastating.

That relationship also caused me so much heartache. He wanted us to get married and said he dreamt about it. His parents gave him so much opposition. I have struggled because he was separated when we met and not divorced. I was a nominal Christian then and should have waited for him to have a final divorce. Though his ex-wife made life difficult, I am sorry for what she must have gone through.

Two major relationships going wrong and then my marriage. Not to mention everything else. I felt I was living under a curse.

On one occasion, I attended a meeting at the Rembrandt Hotel in Knightsbridge with my Connect Group partner, Louis. We were meeting to discuss how we were going to run the Connect Group, goals, mission and so forth. As we were talking, Louis felt an instantaneous sharp headache almost to the point that it felt like a migraine. Considering Louis does not get headaches he knew something was off.

He stopped the meeting and said, "Gita, what's going on with you? I never get these types of headaches, and I am sensing there's lots of witchcraft around you."

I was surprised that he picked it up, but Louis is a very prayerful man, so I confirmed that what he was picking up in the spirit was accurate. As a result of my response, he immediately reconvened the meeting for another day. He asked me if he could pray for me and I agreed wholeheartedly. He said he would fast for three days and would then contact me.

Exactly three days later Louis telephoned, he prayed a powerful prayer and I began to feel the bondage leave me, I was set free, in Jesus name.

# CHAPTER 13

### ✦

## HISTORY REPEATING

In May 2018, a couple of mutual friends told me that Pietro and Matilde had split up.

Ever since Pietro and I separated, these friends would comment on how much he had changed. That he was not the same happy go lucky guy that they had come to know. His persona was not the same. He became miserable and complained constantly. The split was inevitable. A relationship built on deceit is doomed to fail. There can never be trust.

Matilde was just like Helga, an opportunist. When things don't go the way they want or expect, she took off. I had told him she had done well coming from Bow to Chelsea and to be careful that she might run off with someone who had more money than him. The parallels between Ken, Sarah, Helga and Pietro, Matilde and myself were glaring. I always thought there was something weird with the energy in the building and a couple of my friends agree with me.

For a few months before their split I would hear the word, 'Wretched,' whenever I drove past the emporium. I knew what it signified and so wasn't surprised that they had split up, but I was shocked at the way she had left him. Without warning she had taken the two children, (the daughter by

Salva and Pietro's daughter) and wouldn't tell him where they were and had made false allegations against him. There wasn't much sympathy from me at first. It was divine retribution after all.

Approximately five weeks after I heard the news (mid-June) an important looking letter from the equivalent of the Italian Inland Revenue came to my flat for Pietro. I thought I would stick it through his letter box when I had time. A day or so after that I had taken my friend, Donna, to the Chelsea Harbour Club for a spa session and we were driving back down the Kings Road and there he was, just standing outside a bar on Kings Road, The Jam Tree.

He was on the phone and he saw me driving past and he started waving, I waved back. I realized I had his letter, but I was dropping my friend off first. I messaged him, letting him know I had this important looking letter for him. It was agreed I would come back and meet him by the emporium to give it to him.

He met me at my car and I handed it over. Then Andrew, his colleague called him, he was the one Pietro was meeting at the Jam Tree that evening. Andrew wanted to talk to me, so the phone was handed to me. He asked me to join them for a drink.

After initial reluctance I thought, why not? It was a nice evening in June. We walked down the road into the bar and down the steps into the garden at the back where Andrew was waiting for us. We had a drink and were chatting, it was like old times. Pietro didn't know I knew as much as I did until I told him I knew about what had happened between him and Matilde. He wanted to know who had told me but I refused to disclose my source. Long story short I said I knew she had run off without telling him and taken the children and wouldn't tell him where they were living.

Back in May his neighbour had called him at work and asked if he was moving? He said no. The neighbour told him there was a big van taking lots of boxes out of his flat. He had to run home and stop them. Matilde was nowhere in sight but was obviously watching nearby and texted him not to touch her boxes. No apology or explanation. She had left a solicitor's letter and one from herself making allegations. He showed me an email accusing him of things he hadn't done. I asked him what he was doing to defend himself, he clearly didn't realize how serious her allegations were.

He was still in shock about the way she had left him. I was going to help him, I was worried about him and his mental state, God had put me there to help him. Some friends thought I was mad, others thought it was noble after everything that had gone on between us. Most of them did not understand or believe the spiritual side of things. They just saw a husband who had been cheating and got caught. I tried to defend him because I knew he was a spiritual captive.

A few, like my friends at the church knew exactly what I had been up against during the previous two to three years. Louis, Donna, Karina and Charis would pray for my situation and Pietro regularly. This was way before I was speaking to Pietro again. On a couple of occasions when I had been praying with Donna, she had a vision where she saw Pietro wherever he was living and this huge snake had just slithered out of his flat really fast and she felt it wasn't coming back. She also told me she heard the word, 'Innocent' loud and clear. The same word I had received about Pietro in my Sozo in Holy Trinity Swiss Cottage. I hadn't mentioned the Sozo details to Donna, so it was a confirmation to me that Pietro was a victim in all this, of course he made some choices for what happened, but I knew for certain that he was under an influence. Later that afternoon when I was sorting out my clothes to give to charity, I came across a tee-shirt with a big cobra on it, its mouth wide open. I can't remember who gave it to me. I hadn't thrown it away because it was a present. Donna saw it and said it was exactly like the snake she had seen leaving Pietro's home. She said she would take the tee-shirt home with her and throw it away. In fact, she later told me she felt compelled to cut it into pieces first and then threw it in the rubbish.

On another occasion, Donna who had been studying Sozo at Ellel Ministries and I were praying for protection for me late one evening, as I felt I was under massive oppression. As we were praying I had this very clear vision of the real Pietro in a cage desperately pulling at the metal bars trying to get out and he was screaming my name. That prayer came to an abrupt halt because the atmosphere had changed. It became very tense and cold. We needed protection that night. The vision of Pietro in a metal cage, I will never forget it. One instance comes to mind, I attended an event where I spent the day attending a course and doing a Firewalk run by Harun Rabbani. It was a very memorable day and I felt elated that I had walked over burning coals! A friend, Bianca, went with me in the car and we completed the day and she asked me to go to a birthday party of a psychiatrist friend of hers.

We went along to a lovely flat in North London. An Indian man, Suresh, was playing host and I didn't realise until later it was his own flat. The upshot is he suddenly told me while drinking at the table that he was an energy worker/clairvoyant. I was reserved and I wanted to keep my distance. He suddenly declared that my husband has an entity inside him, and he could remove it! I was stunned.

I knew it and so did my other spiritual friends but here was a perfect stranger I had never met or spoken to before. It was so tempting to agree to his fee for doing whatever he was going to do to make this happen. I took his card and put it in my purse. The next day I called Pastor B, told her I was tempted but didn't go through with it.

Concerned about Pietro's situation I rang my solicitor, Karen, who had conducted my divorce and asked her to brace herself as I wanted her to help Pietro now. She was understanding and agreed.

Pietro was all over the place emotionally. We had a lot of unfinished business and it made me emotional too. He kept asking for forgiveness and I told him I had but then some issue would surface that would set me off. This was early June 2018. For weeks I helped him to counter the false allegations that Matilde was making against him and helped him to prepare statements which kept Karen's fees down.

As events were unfolding in Pietro's current drama, the awful truth was dawning on him. Pietro was now going through what Matilde had previously done to Salva, the father of her first child a few years back when Pietro had come onto the scene. She had made very similar allegations of domestic violence against Salva. This was to prevent him from seeing his daughter and he had to jump through hoops for two years before he could gain access to her.

Matilde was so convincing that Pietro had believed everything he had been told about Salva being violent to Matilde. However, she was now making allegations of domestic violence against Pietro which were totally untrue. She had played them both. He was horrified that his reputation was being damaged and that the local authorities were being led to believe that he was violent or abusive to her and the children. The only explanation for her destructive behaviour was that it was not convenient to have her ex's around whenever a new man comes into her life.

Pietro didn't want to stay in the flat where he had lived with Matilde, so I gave him a hand and helped him move into a smaller but swish flat near the emporium. I accompanied him to the police station when they called him in for questioning for the false allegations made against him. We spent a lot of time together trying to sort out his situation.

He said he loved me and wanted to rebuild his life with me. I told him I would help him but that I didn't trust him and that he had just come out of a dysfunctional relationship. One step at a time. My pastors welcomed him back with open arms. They were glad the prodigal son had returned to us.

We telephoned Pastor B, she hadn't spoken to Pietro in years, she told him that he didn't realize just how bad a situation he had been in and how demonic Matilde was and that he had been sitting patting the head of a giant snake all that time. He didn't say much to this. He looked numb when talking to her. It was hard to gauge Pietro's reaction to all of this. Obviously, he was in shock and was depressed by his situation and he said he had made a mistake by getting involved with Matilde. He told me he had had a child with the wrong woman. The facts of her actions spoke for themselves.

Somehow, I got the feeling that he was still deaf and blind on the spiritual level. Also, it can be difficult for people to admit that they got it wrong. We started going to Holy Trinity Brompton church together, as well as going to Pastor B's house for prayer. Pastor B didn't mince her words. She said that Pietro had had a narrow escape and that finally he had the proof of what we had all warned him against. We prayed that he would get his daughter back.

I took him to Louis's Connect group, it was interesting for Louis to finally meet Pietro because he had been praying for me on and off for more than two years. Pietro insisted we go to some of Louis's meetings at his flat. Louis spent a lot of time trying to help Pietro break free from Matilde's witchery. Finally, Pietro was now back on the Skype meetings with Pastor D. However, Pastor D was cautious. He kept telling Pietro that he had to make sure he didn't backslide that it was important to stay with God and not return to the darkness. That worried me, Pastor D doesn't say things without seeing them first. Surely that wouldn't happen. Pietro was so very sorry and seemed to be back to his old self.

I was spending most of my time with him, my mother was thinking I was seeing a new man. Eventually I told her I was helping Pietro and she was very upset. Pastor B had to reassure her I was being a good friend. It was causing arguments at home.

I had heated conversations with the local council because they didn't even check if the allegations were true in Pietro's case. I asked them whether I would get housing straightaway if I claimed I was being abused without providing proof? They hung up on me! A friend of mine spends his time working for a charity to help single fathers, some fathers have been prevented from seeing their children. It's sad to see what goes on in those cases. It turns out that Pietro had been suffering abuse at Matilde's hands. Apparently, she had experienced an abusive childhood, the abused sometimes grow up to abuse. It is a vicious cycle.

Pietro told me that her behaviour had changed in the few months before she left him. She suddenly went on a crash diet, lost lots of weight and was waking up and exercising at 5am in the lounge, putting make-up on and doing her hair before taking the kids to school.

It was obvious to outsiders what was going on. He couldn't see it at the time. It was like he was blinded to what she was doing. I had gone to Portugal for the usual family holiday and he was calling me all the time. Two days before I was due to come back to the UK, I felt a change in the energy. I knew Matilde was staging a comeback as Pastor B put it. Pietro's' cousin, Viola, who was trying to advise him and myself were horrified at what we could see was happening. She even said what I had thought all along, it was a battle of good versus evil. It was a car crash.

I came back and I immediately recognised that Pietro was changing personality again. He had been okay while Matilde's attention was elsewhere but now, he was starting to act strangely again. I was dismayed. My pastors told me to back away. Pastor D had tried to warn me. Pietro had the choice to choose God or go back to the darkness.

In the meantime, not liking once again what our pastors were saying to him, Pietro decided to go to another church who didn't know the whole story and manipulated them to somehow think it was alright for him to go back to Matilde. They were telling him to marry her because they shouldn't be living in sin anymore. Matilde was pretending to Pietro that she had given her life to Christ when she had previously claimed to be a Buddhist. I told Pietro Buddhists are not supposed to harm or kill even the smallest of insects and she had been causing so much damage to everyone she came across.

Pietro had discovered something very unpleasant when we were trying to find out about who the man was that she was seeing. We thought it might be her ex-boyfriend, Salva, so we started investigating. We looked at Salva's girlfriend's Facebook page, there was a post saying, "I like having sex with dead bodies. I am the daughter of Satan and proud of it." It gave us the shivers and it gave me an idea of what Matilde may have been involved with in the past. I had told Pietro to snapshot the post but when he tried to go back in, he had been blocked by Salva.

I could not believe what Pietro was doing now. I know he was trying to protect his daughter. He said he wanted to try and make a go of keeping, 'the family' together. It was complete madness. Pastor B had told him even if he didn't want to believe all the spiritual dark stuff Matilde had been doing to us from the beginning, at least he should look at all the facts and the way she was behaving now. Why would he want to go back to that?

She said to Pietro, "Why would you want to go back to your own vomit?"

Matilde obviously had issues. Why would anyone in their right mind prevent the two fathers from seeing their children and taking such extreme measures? The familiar pattern of him being distraught and not knowing what to do kicked in.

He rang Pastor B very upset, asking her what he should do. He was struggling with the light and the dark again. In the end Matilde's spell binding worked and she didn't want him to speak to me again. In October 2018 he told me not to contact him.

We didn't communicate with each other again until March 2019, at which point he texted me to apologise. So, it must be all off again was all I thought. I tried to remain calm but there is something in me that gets triggered when I know I am up against the devil himself. I lashed out at his stupidity and blindness. It was too hard. I just wanted to know why he kept choosing to go back into darkness.

He didn't want to talk about it. In the end I apologised for my outburst and wished him peace. Only God can deliver him, and he needs to want it. That's how it was left for a few weeks, then strangely enough another official letter for him came to my flat. It was a Friday and I had an extensive travel itinerary scheduled, first I was leaving for Mexico for seven days and then onto India for two weeks. I couldn't remember his new address and decided to drop it to the showroom.

I called him and met him near the showroom as I didn't want to go in. We talked for a while and it was amicable. He was seeing his daughter which was good for him. I still pray for the scales to fall from his eyes. He didn't go for deliverance to Kensington Temple as far as I know. The entity that was inside him may still be there. I still don't think Pietro is himself. He is in God's hands.

I have been rebuilding my life and know I have power and authority, that I am a joint heir with Christ. No weapon formed against me will prosper. There are powerful prayer warriors around me. Anything or anyone wishing harm on me or my loved ones will have their arrows returned to them sevenfold. I am blessed and highly favoured. I want that for everyone. No one should have to suffer or endure spiritual oppression.

Keep your focus upwards.

# CHAPTER 14

—◦◦◦—

## THE GO TO'S

This has been a long journey and in the space of five years a lot of things about myself and what I believe have changed. What drives me is the knowledge that people are going through the same thing that I went through and don't know what to do or where to go. It's important to know that not everything bad that happens to you in life is the result of a spiritual attack. Sometimes life just happens and it's the way it is. Discernment and clarity are important, it is advisable to seek help from those who are more experienced in these matters.

I had been held down for so long and had given my power away. My focus had been misguided on the people and the darkness that was harming me and my loved ones. What you focus on grows. The darkness had latched onto me and I had inadvertently let it in. Ignorance also played its part. I am not a bible scholar or theologian. I am just a normal person with a simple faith.

My belief is that we are made in the image of God, He is in us and we are in Him. Thus, we have His power and authority. I will never allow myself to go down that route again thinking that these evil creatures can harm me. Just as well because my pastor told me that I had so many enemies that it is only God and my strong stance that keeps me going. I laughed because these people must have nothing in their lives so that they spend their time causing trouble for others. My advice to them is get a life!

When challenges come it's best to face them head on. No running away, hiding or procrastinating. Deal with them in the present. You can't change what has already happened. Dwelling on the past is a waste of time and energy. Just as you can't change the person or people that have caused you pain and anger. They have to want to change. If you look to others to make you happy, that may be disappointing. Be happy with yourself and develop a relationship with yourself. Love you. Besides, when people act out or lash out at you, it's not usually about you, it's about them. Hopefully you can learn whatever it is that you were meant to learn from that experience, not repeat the same mistakes and forgive others as well as yourself. And finally, remember the goodness in them and the happy times and move forward with your life.

*Finally, brethren, whatsoever things are true, whatsoever things are honest, whatsoever things are just, whatsoever things are pure, whatsoever things are lovely, whatsoever things are of good report; if there be any virtue, and if there be any praise, think on these things.*

**Philippians 4:8**

I understand that pain is an important part of life. We all experience intense emotional pain at some point or another. It is natural to want to run away from it or avoid it. However, it is there for our growth and expansion otherwise we would be like two-dimensional amoeba. Looking back on my life the greatest leaps in my creativity came after periods of emotional pain. It was hard to embrace it at the time but with everything I am learning I would approach this differently in the future.

Trying not to judge is hard as well as holding onto unforgiveness as it only hurts the person holding onto it. Don't for one second believe that forgiveness is a one-time event. It can take time, and that's ok as long as you are willing to forgive and keep going back and doing it again for as long as it takes. The important thing is to heal yourself and be set free.

With so many good people helping me and with God's grace I learnt to focus on the good and on the light which grew making me feel emotionally lighter. Where there is light there can be no darkness. Choose to, 'Be the Light.'

This part of the book is aimed at giving practical help to anyone who has been suffering from oppression and has been aware of it but has not known what to do or where to go for help. And for those of you for whom the penny has dropped. And you are now questioning – "Is this something that is happening to me?" I am speaking to so many people and when I tell them what the book is about, they say that something strange is going on in their lives and this could now explain it.

If you are sceptical about the existence of opposing forces or any forces operating in the physical and spiritual world please ask questions of yourself and others. We all use electricity which is a hugely powerful energy but can you see it? Just because it can't be seen doesn't mean it doesn't exist. What are we made up of? An outer shell and the spirit within? When the body dies, where is the spirit? Can you see it? This isn't all there is.

## FOR THOSE SUFFERING FROM SPIRITUAL ATTACK AND OPPRESSION

Firstly, how can you tell what the signs and symptoms are which indicate that you may be under witchcraft or demonic possession?

They can usually overlap.

# SIGNS AND SYMPTOMS

Lethargy, drowsiness, fatigue and low energy.

Persistent yawning.

Frequent and sudden headaches.

Voices speaking to you (internal and external).

Changes in personality.

Eye changes (not colour).

Sudden behavioural changes.

Mood swings.

Looking and feeling ill.

Suicidal tendencies.

Everything going wrong in your life.

Bad luck.

Problems with relationships.

Financial blocks or problems.

Business drying up.

Anxiety attacks.

Bouts of depression.

Sleep problems.

Nightmares.

A feeling something is sitting on your chest and/or strangling you.

People acting strangely towards you, turning on you and acting out of character.

Constant arguments and clashing with loved ones over little things as if something is trying to pull you apart.

Manifestations at home.

Strong smells.

Presence of entities/spirit in the home.

Mould or mushrooms growing unexpectedly in the home.

Mental and physical problems.

Accusations,

Seeing things real or imagined.

Sudden stabbing pains.

Nausea, belching and stomach problems.

Sudden changes in feelings towards loved ones. Witchcraft can make people hate the person they are with, or convince them that their partner does not love them anymore. They then, 'fall in love' with the person who is exerting witchcraft on them. They are usually so bound and cannot break away, regardless of how badly they are being treated unless there is major intervention.

People who are demon possessed need deliverance but the spirit inside won't want to come out without a fight as I mentioned before. If they won't go voluntarily for deliverance, once again major intervention is needed.

# HOW TO FIGHT BACK

Realize who you are in Christ. You are strong, mighty and bold. Remember you are a Child of God. *"Do not touch my anointed ones,"* **Psalm 105 v 15.** That is God's warning. People will reap what they sow.

Mindset is very important.

Believe, "No weapon formed against you will prosper," **Isaiah 54 v 17.**

Nothing anyone does against you will work in the end. Adopting a very positive mindset does wonders. I know when you are down in the pit or depressed it is very difficult to see the way out. Listen to your body, if you need to sleep to get through the worst days then sleep. There is nothing worse than other people telling you to pull yourself together and get up and do this or that. But do let your family and friends support you in the way you want. Pamper yourself whenever you can. It doesn't have to cost money e.g. take long hot baths, walk in nature, read good books or watch comedy films.

Remember if you feel someone is putting any form of negative energy on you, they are less evolved than you, little people do little things I was told. You are way bigger than that. My mentor told me when there is chaos around you and problems seem to find you, this is the time to laugh! Laugh at your challenges if you can. I remember obsessing about my problems and that kept me stuck. Take your attention off them. Remember what you focus on grows.

Take time to analyse and think about what is really happening in your life. It really could just be misfortune. If your senses or gut tells you something is wrong, you are usually right. Discernment is important. This is the time to pray and ask the advice of a trusted friend or pastor. This is also when things will be revealed to you. Take responsibility if you have acted poorly or without integrity with certain people in your lives, which is a polite way of saying you have behaved like an idiot towards others and now unpleasant things are happening to you, this could be divine retribution. You have to understand that and deal with it. No denial or playing innocent. And if you have opened the door to the enemy, find the cause because first and foremost, it's you that has to shut it!

When you are aligned to the Creator nothing can touch you, negative things just fly off you. I realise that now and aim to stay in alignment.

## PRAYER

Prayer is a hugely powerful. Spend time alone in prayer and just be. You will get guidance and insights as to what is really happening. Also praying with others especially in agreement is important and comforting. Ask powerful prayer warriors to pray with and for you.

The Lord's Prayer in the Bible: **Luke 11: 2-4** is very simple, short and effective.

Below are two short, empowering prayers by Pastor B.

*Prayer Against Oppression*

I pray in the Name of our Lord Jesus Christ that, henceforth you shall no longer experience oppression in any area of your life. All weapons of the enemies that have been afflicting you shall never prosper again, and everyone interested in or assigned to afflict you shall be permanently frustrated. Every work of satanic sacrifice made to afflict you shall backfire against their sources. This is a prosperous season for you and your life shall arise and shine in Jesus Mighty Name.

*Prayer of Achievement*

I pray that the Lord God Almighty will empower you to outrun all the plans and devices of your enemies. He will empower you and will grant you great speed to achieve and actualise the impossible and cause the desires of your heart to come to pass. It's your season to be announced in Jesus Name.

## CHURCH

If you enjoy going to church, do the research and find the right church that can support you and join groups and activities to build up a support network and like-minded friends.

## SPIRITUAL ATTACK

If you suspect you are under spiritual attack there are churches that may be able to help you. It's prudent to also research who in your area is well versed in deliverance ministry. It is a specialised area and not everyone is anointed to do it. And it can be dangerous, so it is undertaken in teams of two or more people.

Attend Sozo at Holy Trinity Swiss Cottage.

Finchley Road. London NW3 5HT.

0207 644 0083

**www.htsc.org**

Ellel Ministries UK.

Pierrepoint, Frensham, Farnham. GU10 3DL

01252 794060

**www.ellel.org/uk**

There are several international branches.

The Prayer and Healing team at Holy Trinity Brompton in Knightsbridge.

Brompton Road. London SW7 1JA

0845 644 7533

**www.htb.org**

There are many satellite churches.

Online Resources, Books and Videos.

There are plenty of resources that can help you enormously as they did me.

Derek Prince Ministries.

**www.dpmuk.org**

Videos and books.

The book: Blessings or A Curse You Choose.

Gabriel Fernandes Ministries.

**www.gabrielfernandesministries.org**

Powerful Prayers for all areas.

Mountain of Fire and Miracles Ministries (MFM Ministry).

This is a powerful deliverance ministry all over the world.

They have strong prayers on YouTube.

Dr. Olukoya Prayers.

**www.mountainoffire.org**

Cindy Trimm.

Videos, talks and books.

The book: Commanding Your Morning.

**www.cindytrimmministries.org**

TV Ministries.

Joyce Meyer.

**www.joycemeyer.org**

Enjoying Everyday Life TV programme.

Sid Roth.

**www.sidroth.org.**

It's Supernatural TV programme.

## SCRIPTURES

**Psalm 9: 2-4** "I will be glad and rejoice in thee: I will sing praise to thy name, O thou most High.

When mine enemies are turned back, they shall fall and perish at thy presence." **Psalm 9: 5** "Thou hast rebuked the heathen, thou hast destroyed the wicked, thou hast put out their name for ever and ever."

Verse 9.

"The Lord also will be a refuge for the oppressed, a refuge in times of trouble".

Verse 16. "The Lord is known by the judgment which he executeth: the wicked is snared in the work of his own hands."

**Psalm 9: 2-16**

2. I will be glad and rejoice in thee: I will sing praise to thy name, O thou most High.

3. When mine enemies are turned back, they shall fall and perish at thy presence.

4. For thou hast maintained my right and my cause; thou satest in the throne judging right.

5. Thou hast rebuked the heathen, thou hast destroyed the wicked, thou hast put out their name for ever and ever.

6. O thou enemy, destructions are come to a perpetual end: and thou hast destroyed cities; their memorial is perished with them.

7. But the LORD shall endure for ever: he hath prepared his throne for judgment.

8. And he shall judge the world in righteousness, he shall minister judgment to the people in uprightness.

9. The LORD also will be a refuge for the oppressed, a refuge in times of trouble.

10. And they that know thy name will put their trust in thee: for thou, LORD, hast not forsaken them that seek thee.

11. Sing praises to the LORD, which dwelleth in Zion: declare among the people his doings.

12. When he maketh inquisition for blood, he remembereth them: he forgetteth not the cry of the humble.

13. Have mercy upon me, O LORD; consider my trouble *which I suffer* of them that hate me, thou that liftest me up from the gates of death:

14. That I may shew forth all thy praise in the gates of the daughter of Zion: I will rejoice in thy salvation.

15. The heathen are sunk down in the pit *that* they made: in the net which they hid is their own foot taken.

16. The LORD is known *by* the judgment *which* he executeth: the wicked is snared in the work of his own hands. Higgaion. Selah.

## Psalm 23: 1-6 Particularly:

Verse 1.

"The Lord is my shepherd; I shall not want."

Verse 4.

"Yea, though I walk through the valley of the shadow of death, I will fear no evil: for thou art with me; thy rod and thy staff they comfort me."

Verse 6.

"Surely goodness and mercy shall follow me all the days of my life: and I will dwell in the house of the Lord for ever."

## Psalm 27:1-3

"The Lord is my light and my salvation; whom shall I fear? The Lord is the strength of my life; of whom shall I be afraid? When the wicked even mine enemies and foes, came upon me to eat up my flesh, they stumbled and fell. Though an host should encamp against me, my heart shall not fear: though war should rise against me, in this will I be confident."

## Psalm 27: 14

"Wait on the Lord: be of good courage, and he shall strengthen thine heart: wait, I say on the Lord."

# AFFIRMATIONS

These are for encouragement. Here are some examples below.

*I am whole, healthy, perfect, strong, loving, loved, powerful, successful, wealthy, harmonious and happy.*

*I am bold, courageous, strong.*

*I am loving, loved and happy.*

*I am powerful, successful and abundant.*

*Every day in every way I am getting better and better.*

There are many number of combinations you can use to suit your needs or situations.

**Romans 4:17**

You are calling those things unseen as seen or, "calling those things which are not as though they were."

Summon the things that do not yet exist as though they already do.

This is so incredibly powerful. Marry your thoughts with your emotions, see what you desire as being already here/accomplished and give thanks. What you desire has to have integrity and not harm others of course.

The majority of today's great motivational speakers have taken a lot of what they know from teachings that have come from the Bible and packaged them in their own way.

## DECLARATIONS

These are powerful and effective, more so than affirmations.

Decree and declare them frequently.

A few examples below:

*I am divine love and power.*

*I am victorious through Christ.*

*I am set free.*

*I am healed by the stripes of Jesus Christ.*

*I overcome evil.*

*I constantly overcome challenges.*

*My path is straight and clear.*

*I am untouchable and unstoppable.*

You can create your own declarations or use some of the great resources available on the internet.

It is helpful to find mentors who can direct and focus you on getting your life back on track or, to take your mind off things that are dragging you down. They can give you insights on your life's purpose. I have given you the names of my mentors who have helped me greatly so please feel free to look them up.

I truly hope that this book has been helpful and that you will be set free and live happy, healthy and purposeful lives.

### Ephesians 5:8 (KJV)

*[8] For ye were sometimes darkness, but now are ye light in the Lord: walk as children of light.*

Printed in Poland
by Amazon Fulfillment
Poland Sp. z o.o., Wrocław

55030570R00113